BRISTOL MOTOR SPEEDWAY

RACIN' THE WAY IT WAS

Featuring Ten Years at
NASCAR's Most Popular Track

RON L. SCALF

Copyright © 2014 Ron L. Scalf
All rights reserved.

ISBN: 1489516271
ISBN 13: 9781489516275
Library of Congress Control Number: 2014920998
CreateSpace Independent Publishing Platform
North Charleston, South Carolina

CHAPTER 1

Racin' The Way It Was

It has always been my opinion if you want to be a good newspaperman, you have to be married to the job, even though some mornings, you'd rather be back in a warm bed as opposed to going to work. It's 1985 and I'm actually working as Bureau Chief for the *Johnson City (Tenn.) Press* in the next-door sleepy town of Erwin, Tenn., population 3,800. Erwin is sandwiched between Johnson City and the North Carolina mountains near Asheville.

My "promotion" to Bureau Chief came after two years of copy desk work at the *Press'* main office, paying my dues, working a schedule of 4 p.m. to 1 a.m. including weekends and holidays. Working for a newspaper is the only profession I can think of that pays worse than elementary school teachers.

Yet, the Bureau Chief's job also has its advantages, because, on a normal day, (unless there is a school board or town commission meeting to cover after normal working hours) I generally am home by 6 p.m. with weekends off unless a rare murder happens or there is a festival in town. And, it is hard for my supervising editor to look over my shoulder from 20 miles away. I do a lot of street walking and I hang out at the courthouse and local diner, looking for story ideas. It's not a bad gig, considering I come and go as I please and enjoy being outdoors.

My goal in life is to pay off my student loans before I retire, which gives me about 32 years. I have a wife and a young son, who (like me) faces the prospect of going in debt if he plans to attend college when his time rolls around because I certainly can't afford it.

A February snow starts peppering down as I make my morning rounds to the county jail in an attempt to gather information on "who, what, when and where" from the previous night. The county schools are canceled because of snow and the town's lone movie theatre has opened early to cash in on the juvenile population, many of whom have been dropped off by parents who want them "out of their hair" for a while.

Much to this newspaperman's delight on this frosty Monday morning, the jail docket reveals a late-night arrest made in the Flag Pond community after a truck driver came home early to find his wife in bed with his brother. A fight ensued and the trucker stabbed his brother and would be arraigned later in the day in Unicoi County General Sessions Court on charges of attempted first-degree murder. I wondered if the stabbing would be enough to garner some space on the front page – which is always the goal of a reporter working away from the paper's home base.

Back in my cramped office across the street from the courthouse, I hurriedly ate my bagged lunch of a tuna sandwich, chips and a banana. The rest of the day would be spent in the courtroom.

The room used for Unicoi County General Sessions Court is about three times the size of my small bathroom. There are only three rows of seats, capable of accommodating a handful of visitors and members of the press.

Two small mahogany desks are situated in front of the judge's elevated station complete with a lone high-backed black leather chair. Sitting at one of the tables is the assistant district attorney general for the county. The other table is empty for this particular hearing. The state seal of Tennessee is the only wall adornment and a lone artificial green plant guards the door going into the judge's chambers.

At precisely 1 p.m., a burly sheriff's deputy opens the judge's chamber door and bellows, "All rise! Unicoi County General Session Court is now called to order. The honorable Judge Lynn Franklin presiding."

"Please be seated," Judge Franklin said in a barely audible monotone. He knew his job today would only be to "bind over" the accused to a higher court, because his court is solely charged with dealing with misdemeanor cases like DUIs, simple assaults or other so called minor offenses. However, statutorily, General Sessions Court is the first stop in getting the wheels of justice moving.

> "Call your first case, Mr. District Attorney," commands Judge Franklin.
> "Yes, your honor," said the young D.A. in a wrinkled jacket that looks like he's slept in it in his car in the parking lot the night before. "State vs. Billy Joe Willis, attempted first-degree murder." Billy Joe Willis comes through the same door I entered, through a metal detector. He's a big man, 6 foot 4 and 250 pounds. Dressed in a sheriff's department issued orange jump suit, he wears a smirk on his face, handcuffs on his wrists and shackles on his feet. He is escorted by two sheriff's deputies half his size.
> "Mr. Willis were you read your rights?" Judge Franklin asks.
> "Yes, sir," answers Willis with his head bowed.
> "Do you have an attorney, Mr. Willis?"
> "Nope," he says.
> "Can you afford one?" Franklin continues.

"Drive a truck, whaddaya think? "His comment draws a chuckle from the sparse gallery.

Franklin's gavel slams sharply on his desk but he ignores the comment.

"Mr. District Attorney, I've read your complaint and there appears to be provable cause in this case. Pending a review of his finances, Mr. Willis will be appointed a public defender lawyer for his defense. What'll you say to bond?"

"$1 million, your honor. His brother's on life support," the D.A. announces proudly.

"Now, now Fred, the man can't afford gas in his truck and it appears that kinda bond at this point is excessive. I'll set it at $100,000. He ain't going anywhere, anyway."

"Yes, your honor," Fred said, rolling his eyes to the sparse audience away from the judge's view.

"Very well, call your next case."

Rather than wasting another minute hearing one of the dozens of minor cases listed on the docket and obviously of no news value, I follow Willis and the deputies out the door and down the stairs to the parking lot where their cruiser was parked.

"Mr. Willis, I noticed you didn't have much to say up there!" I called out to the trio who were racing off to the black-and-white.

Turning around, Willis asks, "Who the hell are you?"

"Reporter."

"Got nothing to say."

"How's your brother?"

"Fuck you!"

All in a day's work and I couldn't quote Willis in my exclusive story. After all, we were a family newspaper.

My eight paragraph story on the attempted murder of brother vs. brother, with a wife mixed in, landed at the bottom of Page 6, bumped off the front page by a house fire and an announcement by the Johnson City, Tenn. mayor that he would not seek re-election. As always, I protest.

"Ron, it was a preliminary hearing. We'll save you some space when a jury votes to give him the electric chair," says my editor, Brad Jolly. "Brothers have been poking each other's wives for years. Not front page news anymore."

To salvage the day, I write a feature story about a breeder of miniature horses who turned to this particular profession after the bank foreclosed on his apple tree farm. It was picked to be the Features front in the upcoming Sunday edition because the features editor liked the "pretty pictures of the little horses." Tomorrow would be a more exciting day, I try to convince myself. It's the second Friday of the month and the County Commission meets to discuss raising property taxes. Such is the life of a Bureau Chief in a small rural town. But, somebody's gotta do it!

For some reason it didn't seem Saturday would ever roll around. I was looking forward to spending the night watching professional boxing at the Bristol Sports Arena. For the past two years, I had been covering boxing events there for the sports department, even though the only compensation was two ringside seats, so I could see all the action up close with a friend in tow.

No one in the sports department at the newspaper liked boxing and one reporter even declared, "Boxing is not a sport," and, he said, "not one of our readers are interested in the sport since [Muhammad Ali retired]." I thought that comment was a little strange since Larry Carrier, the owner of Bristol International Raceway and the Bristol Sports Arena, seemed to have little trouble filling the place once a month in fall and winter.

That's how I first met Larry Carrier – two years earlier, at his boxing training facility located a mile from the famed Bristol International Raceway, The World's Fastest Half-Mile NASCAR track.

As a lad, my brother and I were amateur boxers in Elizabethton, Tenn., where above a downtown restaurant we trained in my dad's gym every day after school. It was a time in the late 1960s when there were boxing gyms in most small towns all over America. Northeast Tennessee was no exception, and we had regular matches against kids from Kingsport, Bristol and Greeneville. Thus grew my love for the sport – and my attraction to the Bristol Sports Arena and Larry Carrier's boxing promotions once a month.

The first thing I noticed about Larry when I first met him at his training facility was his firm handshake and his youthful-looking face. He looked 50 instead of 60 – something he later attributed to a leading a wholesome life (after some wild partying times in his younger days). His diet now consisted of not drinking alcohol or smoking, eating large portions of vegetables and getting plenty of sleep, although I would later learn that he regularly stayed up past midnight. His boxing training facility and Sports Arena were colorfully decorated with pictures of famous boxers, many of which were personally signed to: "My good friend Larry."

I gave little thought to the colossal NASCAR racing facility as I meandered down the winding road to the Sports Arena to yet another press conference/interview session with this day's seven local boxers. Seven fighters were featured at the facility once a month as part of the Budweiser Saturday Night Fights.

I found it odd, however, that Larry landed such a well-known international sponsor and yet you couldn't find a Bud within 10 miles of the place. I guess that is why management occasionally had to escort out of the facility someone who had consumed too many libations at one of the many bars and restaurants in Bristol or Johnson City prior to the boxing event.

Entering the building with members of the local press corps was always a treat for me. I once asked Larry, an accomplished amateur boxer in his own right, if he preferred promoting boxing over NASCAR racing. "Boxing is like golf," he said matter-of-factly. "You either like it or you don't. And, like golf, if you box, you are in the arena and the ring all by yourself. This ain't a team sport and your success lives in your ability to throw punches and not take them."

And NASCAR racing? "To be honest I liked the old days and was a friend of 'Fireball' Roberts because he was aggressive on any track and never gave up – kinda like Dale Earnhardt [Sr.] today," he said. "If you're a good boxer, you can succeed without a lot of money. In NASCAR, if you don't have at least $5 million to dedicate to running a season, forget about it. You'll never be able to run up front. Fact is there are maybe 10 out of 42 drivers that can and will win on Sunday. As a NASCAR promoter, I'd like to see someone different win every week because it keeps the sport interesting and the drama bleeds over to the next race."

Enter Mark Carrier, Larry and Shirley Carrier's son, an up-and-coming heavyweight boxer who could punch a hole in a galvanized garbage can lid at close range. At this point in his career, his record is 12-1 with 11 knockouts and his lone loss came in a highly controversial four-round split decision in his third fight that he later avenged.

Mark stands 6-foot-2, weighs about 220 and has boyish good looks. He's still a kid. He's also the main draw at the Bristol Sports Arena. I've noticed the only time there were empty seats in the arena was when Mark was not in the lineup. There were also (admittedly) two types of people who came to see Mark Carrier box: a majority who wanted to see him win and the jealous others who yearned for his failure.

Ironically, besides boxing, Mark enjoyed NHRA/IHRA drag racing, where drivers travel over 200 mph down a quarter-mile track in seconds, as opposed to NASCAR racing inside the Bristol bowl or super speedways like Talladega or Daytona where the races last two to three hours. After all, he grew up watching his dad promote events at the Bristol Dragway and was educated on Larry's International Hot Rod Association (IHRA) sanctioning body. There was just nothing more exciting to him than seeing a dragster zipping down the quarter-mile track at speeds in excess of 200 mph. And, you didn't have to watch a bunch of cars going around in a circle for three hours finding out who the winner was.

Much to the delight of the members of the press with cameras, Mark was putting on a sparring exhibition against a wiry veteran who was brought to training camp to show the "lad" what happens when a boxer steps up to boxing more rounds and against better competition.

With headgear in place and wearing oversized 18-ounce gloves (12-ounce gloves are used in professional competition for heavyweights), Mark dropped the experienced vet three times in less than five minutes, and the last time I saw this guy, he was heading back to Atlanta on a Greyhound bus.

Later in the week, inside the boisterous packed house at the Bristol Sports Arena, Mark Carrier earned his 13th win and another knockout. A black-and-white photo of Mark looking over his shoulder, admiring his work as his opponent lay knocked out face-up on the canvas, won a local newspaper photographer "Best Sports Photo" at the Associated Press annual awards.

And, for the record, the other six local boxers on the card also won their bouts. Life was good in Bristol, Tenn. It was a long night and I drove straight home and enjoyed several Buds – after looking all night at that logo in the ring.

CHAPTER 2

There Was Something About The Call

I was just back from my daily routine of checking the latest crime activity from the night before at the Unicoi County Jail when Tiffany, my clerk/secretary, said I had a phone call on Line 2. "Says his name is Richard Christmas," she says matter-of-factly.

Richard happened to be Mark Carrier's personal boxing trainer at the Bristol Boxing Training Facility. He was a veteran match-maker/trainer with decades of experience, a Jack-of-all-trades when it came to the sport of professional boxing. He was a likable fellow, in his late 60s, but he looked much younger. Every time I saw him at the training gym in Bristol he was spitting out pistachio shells. Richard was from Cleveland, Ohio. We had that connection, because some of my aunts and uncles were from Cleveland, and my Dad left Tennessee in the late 1950s to work at a Goodrich tire plant in neighboring Akron because there were no jobs in Elizabethton, Tenn.

.s fond of Richard. He was comical and you gotta love the name. ght?

"What's up, 'Big Man?' "
I always called him Big Man because he was, literally – all 6-foot-5 and 250 pounds of him.
"Boss wants to see you," he bellows into the phone.
"Really? What about?" I ask.
"Just said to come over to the track after lunch. Didn't tell me nothin.' Probably about boxing ... He didn't say, just told me to call you. Said come 'round about 2."
"Okay," I said. "I'll be there."

I left Erwin about 1:15 p.m., remembering what my Dad had always said about important appointments like this one, which was, "Don't be late and don't be on time. Be 10 minutes early." And I was.

Carrier's office was in the same place it had been built in the '60s at the front of the race track entrance but remodeled several times. He had a back entrance to his office at the speedway so people wouldn't know if he was there or not. He was a very private person, a devoted family man to his wife, Shirley, and his boys, Mark and Andy, and he kept to himself except for interaction with a few close friends and confidants.

Despite my father's advice – which Larry obviously didn't hear – I waited in the outside area between his office and the Bristol Raceway ticket office about 45 minutes before his secretary, Evelyn Hicks, summoned me to Carrier's office door, saying, "Larry will see you now."

I rapped on the door and heard a "Come on in," from Mr. Carrier. At this point, he wasn't yet "Larry" to me.

While on the telephone deep in conversation, he motioned me to take a seat in one of the powder blue leather-backed chairs in front of his massive mahogany desk. And, he just kept on talking with one foot, in a cowboy boot, propped up on his desk, which he kept spying like he was trying to line something up.

He finally hung up and greeted me with a hearty handshake and a broad smile and the conversation went something like this:

> "Wondering why you are here again, I'm guessing," he says.
> "Yeah, kind of," I say. "But I was thinking on the drive over here you probably want some press help with the big boxing show you're promoting at Viking Hall next month. I'm game."
> "Naw. This is about the speedway. Looking for somebody," he says.
> "To do what?" I ask.
> "Need a PR man. Fired the last one," he says, calmly looking out the window with his hands folded behind his back.
> "Well, I'll ask around and let you know," I say, getting up from my seat.
> "So, you would be interested in the job?" he asks.
> "Nope. I am not a race fan, don't follow the sport, and if Richard Petty walked through the door I wouldn't know who he was."
> "Well, that's actually a really good trait, because you won't be giving my tickets and press passes away to all your friends, and you'd have your head on straight."
> "My friends are Tennessee football fans and wouldn't ask me to come to the NASCAR races anyway," I blurt out.
> "And, what's my head is being on straight got to do with any thing?" I think.
> "Really? Well, give it a little thought and call me back next week," he says.

Next week came and Richard Christmas calls again. "Boss wants to see you!" comes the familiar voice on the phone to the *Johnson City Press* Erwin Bureau on a late and cold Friday afternoon in February.

> "Ain't got time, Richard. Heading to a hot tub in Pigeon Forge with my girlfriend. Maybe next week."
> "OK, but he wants to talk to you again."
> "I'll call," I say. And, "Sure. Next week, give me a call. Looking forward to the [boxing] show in a couple of weeks!"

Sure enough, Monday morning, the phone was ringing when I arrived at my office. "Ron," Richard Christmas says in the low Southern drawl he had acquired over the last six months, living in a trailer behind the racetrack and serving as Mark Carrier's boxing trainer.

> "Yeah, Boss, what's up?"
> "Laaaarry wants to talk to you today. He said it was important, so can you come over after lunch?"
> "This about that boxing show?"
> "Don't know. He don't tell me nothing. Think he knows we are friends. That's all. Why I call all the time."
> "Geez. OK. I'll be there at 2."

This time, because of past experiences, I leave my office at 2 p.m. and get to the speedway 45 minutes late. Ms. Hicks, not smiling this time, takes me straight to Mr. Carrier's office door. "He's waiting for you," she says and she turns and leaves. I rap on the door.

> "Come on in," he says. "Have a seat."
> Here we go again.
> "You know the Valleydale 500 Winston Cup race is in six weeks?" he says.
> "Nope. Didn't have a clue."

"I want you do be my PR man and I need an answer now. You can also help with the boxing at the Sports Arena."

Suddenly I was somewhat interested.

So, I begin my spiel: "Mr. Carrier, I don't want to be a smart ass or anything but like I said, I'm not your guy. I'm not into NASCAR but I am intrigued about how you get thousands of people to come over here only a few miles from Bluff City and Piney Flats and give you $100 bills to see 36 cars go around in a circle for three hours, eat hamburgers and drink a lot of beer. Business-wise that is truly amazing to me."

He was silent for the longest time to the point I was squirming a bit.

"OK," he finally says. "What'll it take for you to come to work here as my PR man?" (Old school he was.)
"Mr. Carrier."
"Call me 'Larry.' Ain't no Misters in my family."
"Larry," I said beginning to brag as follows: "I am the Bureau Chief in Erwin, Tenn., for the *Johnson City Press*. I am probably, in my opinion, third in position to be the managing editor and run the place one day. And, I'd have you know that they pay me a hefty $21,000 a year, a gas allowance, health care, retirement and I come and go as I please. But that's not for broadcast. I have a young son and a reasonable child support payment. I'm very happy where I am, but thanks for thinking about me for this position. Obviously, I will help you any way possible, promoting your boxing events."

He starts laughing.

"So you want to cut to the chase do you and so do I. Take the job and I will double your salary, pay your insurance, let you pick out a new car from our Ford sponsor every year, give you a gas credit card and an American Express card to entertain the press and sponsors, within reason of course, and you can also promote the boxing shows at the Bristol Sports Arena. But, I ain't having this conversation with you again. You make your mind up right now. And, as far as that newspaper you work for: I don't think they give a damn about you and you'll find that out when you quit tomorrow. I see no need in giving a notice. Do you?"

My heart sank. From $21,000 to $42,000 in an instant? And all that other stuff? Seemed like too good to be true. So I asked for 24 hours to think about it.

"OK," Carrier says. "See you on the job Wednesday."

And, I was there that Wednesday and for the next 10 years – until he sold it to Bruton Smith. Larry Carrier, in my opinion, was the greatest person anyone could have worked for. That's not to say we didn't have many "spirited discussions" and some disagreements but it's to say that work became a commitment to our families and more than just a job. I just never thought he got the credit he deserved.

And, in the end, it was hard not to become a NASCAR fan. In addition, while my job as vice president/general manager of Bristol Motor Speedway became the envy of thousands, I never saw it that way. It was a great job, but on any given day, it was still a job at a racetrack in Bristol, Tenn. And I never forgot that.

CHAPTER 3

My first live racing experience

Larry Carrier first offered me free Bristol NASCAR race tickets and a seat in his private glassed-in suite in 1985. I was covering his boxing events and we quickly became friends. As I have said, I wasn't a race fan but marveled at the crowds going to NASCAR Winston Cup races at Bristol International Raceway. I graciously declined and even forgot to tune in to the action on television. I was more interested in the progress of the New York Yankees at training camp – that opened the same week as the spring events at the speedway – and in boxing champion Mike Tyson.

I did read the racing results days later in my office at the *Johnson City Press'* Erwin Bureau. I remember that in spring 1988, Bill Elliott won the Valleydale Meats 500, driving the Coors Ford. I chuckled at the title of the race at the time. The popular "Man In Black" Dale Earnhardt, piloting the black No. 3 GM Goodwrench Chevrolet, won the fall night race. People tied to racing said Earnhardt would either go around you, through you or over you to win a race. I thought he'd make a great prize fighter.

In early February 1989, when I was hired as BIR public relations director (and elevated to vice president/general manager a year later) I thought I had better learn a thing or two about NASCAR. In those days, you couldn't turn on a computer and Google "NASCAR" or "Bristol International Raceway" and get a wealth of information and answers, as you can now. So, I spent a week or two at the Johnson City Public Library, near my house, reading up on the sport I knew nothing about.

I found some history of NASCAR from an old racing book. It's now on their web site:

What is NASCAR, I asked myself? I soon found out from old manuscripts and newspaper articles on microfilm. Established in 1947, NASCAR has grown to become the premier motorsports organization.

The National Association for Stock Car Auto Racing (NASCAR) was "born" after a December 1947 meeting at the Streamline Hotel in Daytona Beach, Fla., where Bill France Sr. sought to organize the growing sport. What grew from this summit of automotive leaders was a national phenomenon, now in its seventh decade of racing.

France's vision to bring stock car racing under one organization has seen the sport transition from the dusty, dirt tracks and sandy beaches of its earliest days to today's high-tech speedways and television coverage that broadens its reach to millions of fans.

France helped facilitate that growth with the construction and 1959 debut of Daytona International Speedway, which hosts the sport's crown jewel race – the Daytona 500 – every February on its steep asphalt banks.

The NASCAR Sprint Cup Series, which was born as the "Strictly Stock" division in 1949, is now the premier motor sports circuit in North America. The sport has gone from racing the modified, pre-World War II coupes of bygone eras to competing with the brand-new sixth generation of stock car – aggressively styled, purpose-built racers derived from road-going Chevrolet, Ford and Toyota sedans.

Three national series, four regional touring series, one local grassroots series and three international circuits race under the NASCAR banner, which also sanctions the International Motor Sports Association (IMSA) series.

The vivid history of the sport has a home in the NASCAR Hall of Fame, which opened in 2010 in Charlotte, N.C. The family business continues to thrive today under the leadership of grandson Brian Z. France, NASCAR chairman and CEO, and granddaughter Lesa France Kennedy, who serves on the NASCAR board of directors.

The National Association for Stock Car Auto Racing Inc. is the sanctioning body for one of North America's premier sports. NASCAR races are broadcast in more than 150 countries and 20 languages. In the U.S., races are broadcast on FOX, TNT, ABC/ESPN/ESPN2, SPEED, Motor Racing Network Radio, PRN Radio and Sirius XM Satellite Radio. NASCAR fans are among the most brand-loyal of all sports, and as a result, more Fortune 500 companies participate in NASCAR than any other sport.

NASCAR consists of three national series – the NASCAR Sprint Cup Series, NASCAR Nationwide Series and NASCAR Camping World Truck Series – four regional series and one local grassroots series, as well as three international series.

Also part of NASCAR is IMSA, known for its competition on road courses with multiple classes of cars. NASCAR sanctions more than 1,200 races at 100 tracks in more than 30 U.S. states, Canada, Mexico and Europe. Based in Daytona Beach, Fla., NASCAR has offices in eight cities across North America.

In 1989, most of the racing information I could find was in individual biographies, written by ghostwriters about particular popular drivers, such as Fireball Roberts and Richard Petty. I did find articles in the local newspapers about the history of Bristol International Raceway, Larry Carrier's involvement with NASCAR and the fact that he was also the founder of the International Hot Rod Association (IHRA). I read that behind the oval track of the main Bristol Raceway Carrier had built a drag strip where IHRA races were held, and that he had done the same at another dozen tracks across the country.

In fact, history shows that drag racing in the late 1960s and '70s was more popular than NASCAR. I found that hard to believe because I had seen photos and television clips of the huge crowds at the Daytona 500, Talladega and even at Bristol. I marveled additionally at the allure of two drag cars, side-by-side, roaring down a quarter-mile straightaway at 300 mph for 15 seconds. At the time, a ticket to that spectacle was about $50 a day, which in today's dollars would be equivalent to $200. I guess I never fancied drag racing, either.

February and March passed with painful slowness as did the several cold fronts coming though East Tennessee.

Finally Saturday April 8, 1989, arrived amid a steady rain. As public relations director I would be high above the track on the top floor of the press box for the 200-lap Budweiser Busch Grand National race, along with 30-plus reporters from all over the United States. The Saturday event, I thought, would be good practice for the Valleydale 500 Winston Cup race set for the next afternoon.

A few years later, we added 50 more laps to the race as added entertainment value for our fans. We kept the ticket price low, even though by adding laps, we had to increase the purse for the drivers.

From my front-row position inside the glass-front building of the press box, I could see for miles, and the mountains were absolutely beautiful even through pouring rain. It was obvious why race fans picked Bristol as their favorite NASCAR track. You were right on top of the action no matter where you sat, and, with 32 cars (later we added another four) flying around the steep-banked half-mile oval at 120 mph, this presented the perfect environment for beating and banging of bumpers and flaring tempers.

Ironically, having anticipated this day for months, the 1989 Budweiser 200 was rained out, and we were forced to reschedule the race for the following Monday. Sunday belonged to the Winston Cup boys and as I've said before, the Busch Grand National division was designed for up-and-coming drivers to get experience before jumping over to the big league of NASCAR racing, the Winston Cup [cigarette] series.

A small fortune was made on the Busch races at Bristol and elsewhere but when one is postponed and runs on the following Monday, you can throw that theory out the window. People left the track that Sunday after the Valleydale 500 like their houses were on fire.

In a 30-car field on Monday, April 10, Rick Wilson edged out Mark Martin for the Busch Grand National win. The stands were almost empty.

The preceding day, Sunday, April 9, however, was quite successful for BIR and successful in completely changing my perceptions of racing. Thirty-two drivers took the green flag for the Valleydale Meats 500. Mark Martin set a track record in his Stroh's Light Ford with a qualifying speed of 120.278 mph. There were 34 lead changes among 16 drivers and 20 caution flags for 98 laps. It was a race featuring three-and-a-half hours of door-to-door banging and a multitude of wrecks that saw eight drivers knocked out of contention. I had never seen anything like this before in my life. I had become a fan of the sport and thought this wasn't such a bad gig after all.

The race was a sellout as 67,000 rabid NASCAR fans got their money's worth and then some. The purse was $441,167 and the nice thing about selling all your tickets is the fact the money was in the bank months prior to the event.

Rusty Wallace barely held off Darrell Waltrip for the win with a margin of victory of only 6 seconds. Wallace would win eight more times at Bristol, and even though he didn't win this time, Waltrip would set the record for the most wins at Bristol with 12.

CHAPTER 4

Bristol International Raceway History

As co-owner/founder of Bristol International Raceway, Carl Moore explained the re-named Bristol Motor Speedway could very easily have opened in 1961 under a different name. The first proposed site for the speedway was in Piney Flats, TN., near where a Food City supermarket, fast food restaurants and strip malls stand today. But the idea met local opposition. So the track that could have been called Piney Flats International Speedway was built 5 miles (8.0 km) down the road on U.S. Highway 11-E at the Bristol, TN. city limits. The land upon which Bristol Motor Speedway is built was formerly part of Gray's Dairy, at one point one of the largest dairies in the eastern half of the United States. Larry Carrier met Moore at Charlotte Motor Speedway in 1960 to watch a race and it was then that they decided to build a speedway in northeast Tennessee. However, they wanted a smaller model of CMS, something with a more intimate setting, and opted to erect a .5-mile facility instead of mirroring the massive 1.5-mile track in Charlotte. "I put two dimes together and that was our design," Carrier once told me. "The high banks were to assure there would be much beatin' and banging because of the proposed high banking and narrowness of the race track."

Work began on what was then called Bristol International Speedway in 1960 and it took about one year to finish. Carrier, Moore, and contractor R. G. Pope scratched many ideas for the track on envelopes and brown paper bags. "We'd even personally drive on it as dirt was moved and make note," Carrier said. "Good thing the walls weren't constructed yet because I would have smashed right into them trying to determine the layout and banking during the construction process."

Purchase of the land on which BMS now sits, as well as initial construction of the track, cost approximately $600,000 which would be millions of dollars by today's standard. The entire layout for BMS covered 100 acres and provided parking for about 12,000 cars. The track itself was a perfect .5 miles measuring 60 feet wide on the straightaways, 75 feet wide in the turns, and the turns were banked initially at 22 degrees. Seating capacity for the very first NASCAR race at BMS – held on July 30, 1961 – was a reportedly 18,000. Prior to this race, the speedway hosted weekly races in an effort to bring in extra cash as well as interest from local drivers and fans.

The first driver on the track for practice on July 27, 1961 was Tiny Lund in a Pontiac. The second driver out was David Pearson. Fred Lorenzen won the pole for the first race at BMS with a speed of 79.225 mph. Atlanta's Jack Smith won the inaugural event – the Volunteer 500 – at BMS. However, Smith wasn't in the driver's seat of the Pontiac when the race ended. Smith drove the first 290 laps then had to have Johnny Allen, also of Atlanta, take over as his relief driver. The two shared the paltry $3,225 purse. The total purse for the race was $16,625. Country music star Brenda Lee, who was 17 years old at the time, sang the national anthem. A total of 42 cars started the first race at BMS with only 19 taking the checkered flag.

In the fall of 1969 BMS was reshaped and re-measured. The turns were increased in banking at 36 degrees thus, it became a 0.533-mile oval.

During hard times, the speedway was sold after the 1976 season to businessmen and stock car racing enthusiasts Lanny Hester and Gary Baker. In the spring of 1978 the track name was changed to Bristol International Raceway. In August of that year, the first night race was held on the track, one that would become one of the most popular and highly anticipated events on the NASCAR Sprint Cup Series calendar besides the Daytona 500.

Carrier explained that on April 1, 1982 Lanny Hester sold his half of the speedway to Warner Hodgdon. On July 6, 1983, Hodgdon completed a 100 percent purchase of Bristol International Raceway, as well as Nashville Speedway, in a buy-sell agreement with Baker. Hodgdon named Larry Carrier as the track's general manager. On January 11, 1985, Hodgdon filed for bankruptcy. Afterward, Larry Carrier formally took possession of the speedway and covered all outstanding debts. "I had bills ranging in the thousands of dollars to a bill from a local hardware store for $26 for nails. I made damn sure they all got paid," Carrier once told me. "Our reputation was back on track and we slowly began the process of not only rebuilding that reputation but focusing on what the race fans wanted to see and do when they got to Bristol. And, that meant a lot of work all over the facility. More parking, more bathrooms, more concession stands and more seating."

Carrier was bothered for years by the fact race teams were not able to park their transporters inside the infield, nor did the track have any significant garage area. And, the narrow pits were small and located on both sides of pit road instead of normally having one pit road located on the front stretch. Transporters were parked in a lot outside of the track. During racing periods, crews and participants were landlocked by the track and thus unable to return to the transporters for spare parts, repairs or to get some rest. During my tenure in the early 1990s, the infield was reconfigured and completely paved. Teams began parking the transporters in an orchestrated, extremely tight arrangement that took several hours, and highly skilled drivers, to accomplish. Teams began to be able to work out of their transporters in the same fashion at other facilities.

"The crews and drivers came by my office to thank me for bringing the track up to the expectation of NASCAR and we needed to this to remain a viable racetrack," Carrier once said. "We turned the infield into a place where all the drivers could work on their race cars and not be concerned that they had parts stored outside the track. Because, once the cross-over gate was closed you could not leave the track for fear of not being able to get back in. The cross-over gate, located at Turn 2, would only be opened during a red flag caution or during a hard rain stopping the race."

Larry and I also met with officials from Goodyear Tires and Rubber Company and determined it would be best for us to build them a free-standing building in the infield to house all the tires for the drivers whose crew members would come by individually and sign for their allotment at each race. Each team was responsible for paying its own "tire bill" and each only got so many tires for each race. This led to a practice of race teams buying tires (usually late in the race) from other teams that had been eliminated and had some left. I really never thought that practice was fair because many race teams were on a tight budget and many times were lucky they made it into the field let along be able to afford additional tires if they found themselves in contention.

In 1992, Carrier abandoned the asphalt surface that had been in use since its inception, switching to the all-concrete surface it is now famous for. Soon after the dramatic surface change from asphalt to concrete, the general manager and his staff from Dover Downs International Speedway, Dover, Delaware visited the track to inspect the surface because, they too, were having similar problems with their asphalt surface and was seeking a remedy. Eventually, Dover Downs' "Monster Mile" also became an all-concrete track. I know their visit to BIR had much to do with that decision.

"Maybe that is vindication for my decision at the time," Carrier said later. "I caught hell from everyone over the decision to concrete it but then here comes another track owner who thinks my idea is brilliant. So much so ... he does the same thing. But, at the time I wasn't looking for vindication. I was looking for a solution to my track problem."

Credit: Historical information supplied by NASCAR

CHAPTER 5

At Bristol, The Fans Love The Beatin,' Bangin' & The Fights

As vice president and general manager at Bristol Motor Speedway, it did not take me long to realize that NASCAR fans bought tickets to our racing events to see wrecks, beating and banging, side-by-side racing and the fights – and a helmet-throwing episode occasionally for good measure.

For the nearly 10 years I was there, we had it all. The narrow straightaways, high banks and dizzying quick turns made for all kinds of wrecks and caution flags as 36 sleek and sophisticated aerodynamic stock cars zipped around the track in less than 17 seconds. This was Bristol. Spring or fall, it didn't matter. It became the track that [now retired] racer Jeff Gordon described as "like flying jet airplanes in a gymnasium."

Then the unthinkable happened – a boring race at Bristol! Well, it happens!

It occurred April 5, 1992, at the Food City 500. Round and round the cars went for a little over three hours. The 63,300 fans "only" witnessed 10 cautions for 75 laps and only "a few" spectacular wrecks. Bristol was accustomed to offering its fan base a great racing weekend, time and time again, but this particular weekend was a yawner at the World's Fastest Half-Mile Track.

Although Alan Kulwicki was able to hold off Dale Jarrett by .78 seconds, that was the typical margin of victory for the four or five drivers running vying for the lead at the end of the race. But this time Dick Trickle finished fifth and Hut Stricklin was eighth! Who?

Only 10 caution flags and 11 lead changes among seven drivers: This was not the Bristol "norm."

To make matters worse, popular drivers and big draws such as Dale Earnhardt, Darrell Waltrip, Davey Allison, Bill Elliott, Mark Martin and Richard Petty didn't even finish in the Top 10.

I walked through the stands as I normally did, trying to gauge fan reaction and they weren't happy with "the show," and to be honest, they were more than a little hacked off after shucking out $67 per ticket – and I had to sympathize with them.

No one, however, was more concerned than Larry Carrier. Although he said nothing after the event, I could tell he was ill. We suddenly had a problem, because, you see, racing at Bristol isn't about going around in a circle for three hours. It's about beatin' and bangin' for three hours and drivers taking a last-minute chance for the checkered flag. It seemed to always happen ... but not this time. No drama. No cussing. No helmet throwing. No fights. Just 36 cars going 'round and 'round.

A day after the April racing events I collected my $5,000 cash bonus envelope and went home to sleep for a few days, watch TV and drink some good Scotch. While I was living as a college student in New York

City, I was forced to learn to cook, and cooking to me had become quite therapeutic. So, I dropped a couple hundred dollars at Food City on my way home in anticipation of my local mini-vacation complete with an assortment of steaks, lobster and pasta.

I, however, was still sick about the race weekend. There just wasn't the normal Bristol glee – but events would soon turn that temporary fact around.

On the fourth (and last) day of my self-imposed vacation after the spring racing events, the phone rang at 2 a.m. The conversation went something like this:

> "Hello," I say in a barely audible groggy voice.
> "Ron, it's Larry. What's you doin?"
> "I'm frigging sleeping. What do you think I'm doing?"
> "Well, get over to the track right now and meet me in the pits!" he commands.
> "What the hell is going on that I have to meet you in the infield in the middle of the night?" I ask.
> "Never mind," he says. "Just get your ass over here."
> The line goes dead.

So, I climb out of bed and shove on a pair of wrinkled jeans and a New York Yankees pullover. My head throbs from too much red wine and Scotch not too many hours before. I finally find my keys to the pace car and settle in for the 17-mile jaunt from Baxter Street in Johnson City to the epicenter of Bristol Motor Speedway – in the middle of the night. Incidentally, I kept my Happy Days house shoes on. Thanks, Fonzie.

The night was eerily calm and warm for the time of year. A bright half-moon kissed moving clouds. "Hmm," I thought, "being awakened in the middle of the night is not so bad after all."

With no traffic to speak of, I shoved the pedal to the metal on the Ford Thunderbird Pace Car and reached 90 mph as I passed Winged Deer Park and Boone Lake. As I cruised through Piney Flats, I had a chuckle at the red light, thinking, "This place could have housed the racetrack."

Bristol Motor Speedway was totally dark as I approached the front parking lot and maneuvered to the crossover gate at Turn Three to commence into the track's infield. I had no clue what Carrier was up to, but I didn't ever ask questions unless I was invited to. He signed my checks on Friday and that was good enough for me.

Entering the track in the middle of the night was both strange and inviting. I can still remember the scene. I stopped for a moment to look at those thousands of empty aluminum seats against a backdrop of millions of stars and the clouds "racing" across that beautiful spring moon. "An unpainted Norman Rockwell painting," I thought.

As I scampered into the pit area, I spied Carrier, talking with four men who I recognized as our maintenance guys, like stoic statues among four portable raised halogen light stands like the ones you'd see at a football games or concerts. I pulled the pace car away from them into the far end of the pits and approached on foot.

> "What's up, Boss?" I ask.
> Without a salutation, Carrier gets right to the point as he normally does in situations such as this. "'Member the last race?" he asks.
> "Well, hell yeah," I say. "You know what? I think we would agree ... It sucked!"
> "Whatever. That's in the past. I think I have the solution," he says.
> "Really?"
> "Yeah, really."
> "Follow me," he says.

At the end of the pits facing Turn 1, Carrier hands me an expandable ruler.

"Take that ruler and go up the track 16 inches from the yellow foul line and mark the spot with this paint brush," he says as he hands me a 12-inch-wide paintbrush dripping with white paint.

I do as I'm told, nearly falling down the 38-degree steep bank in the dark.

"OK. Now, what the hell is this all about?" I shout.
"Who's my general manager?"
"Me."
"Well, if you are going to run this place, you need to know important things about what we're doing tonight – here in the middle of the night, as you said," he says with a smile.
"Which is?"
"That little yellow line at all the race tracks is the foul line drivers cannot go under unless they are entering or exiting the pits for cautions or else they are penalized at least a lap," he says. "I'm guessing you, as general manager of my racetrack, have determined it's wise to now move that line up the track 16 inches – which you just marked. Is that correct?"
"We can't move the 'foul line,' " I retort. "That's a NASCAR call. And, if you or your general manager did, that would mean the cars racing here would be more apt to hit the wall and cause wrecks and cautions because it would make this already-steep and narrow race track even closer to those walls for them."
"So what you're saying is we should send these painters – who are prepared to blacken out the existing yellow line tonight with black paint to blend into the pit area and move it up 16 inches where you marked the new caution/foul line to be – home? Mr. General Manager?"
I thought for the longest minute and, realizing the possible race results, said, "I'm exceedingly glad you discovered the problem

with the track, Larry. The August Bud 500 certainly will be exciting. See you in the morning."

As I drove back home that night, it dawned on me that if NASCAR had known what we just did, Carrier would have probably lost his sanctioning. There was never another boring race as long as I was the so-called "general manager," and I was never again called out to the track in the middle of the night.

Until now, that particular secret lasted nearly two decades.

CHAPTER 6

Sponsorships, a Big Money-Maker

I'm guessing that the average race fan doesn't really know where the money ended up after an event at Bristol International Raceway or at other tracks, for that matter. I'll try to explain in layman's terms, based on my tenure.

Track owners, such as Larry Carrier, receive the major portion of television revenue [after production costs] from ESPN's broadcasts, as well as revenue rights for radio sponsorship controlled by Motorsports Racing Network (MRN). That money was vital because it offset the purse or money offered for drivers to race in the event. For example, if you started a race and drove only one lap, you still got paid a couple thousand dollars. Track owners negotiate their own television and radio contracts – thus, our connection with ESPN. At the time, their offer for the TV rights was impressive however, the radio broadcast rights was "chump change" compared to television but the added exposure, we thought, was also a necessity and allowed us another far-reaching opportunity to attract new race fans.

Sponsorships, a Big Money-Maker

The other obvious large revenue stream(s) come from the sales of tickets and proceeds from the many concession stands throughout the facility. Next come rent revenue from all the vendor trailers plus a percentage of each driver's profits derived from the sale of hats, T-shirts and other memorabilia. You may notice the most popular drivers have the best vendor parking at NASCAR tracks. They pay premium "rent" for it.

Thousands of dollars are derived from parking, hospitality tents, billboards, banners and the sale of the event programs, which at Bristol, I helped edit.

NASCAR receives nothing from these revenue streams. Instead, they receive what's called a "sanctioning fee" or the sale of the promotional rights to track owners for each NASCAR event. And, that fee ain't cheap. I can tell you that!

Finally, the naming of the race event can put hundreds of thousands of dollars – now millions – into the track promoter's pocket. This brings me to the Valleydale Meats 500 NASCAR spring race. During my first week at BIR, I was introduced to the owners of Valleydale since their race was only three months away. Valleydale, at the time, was headquartered across the state line in Bristol, Va. They had meat-packing plants that produced bacon, hot dogs, frozen chili, bologna and other packaged meat products, which were shipped locally and as far away as Russia.

Valleydale was in the midst of a three-year sponsorship agreement with BIR totaling $225,000, $75,000 for each year's title rights to the Valleydale 500 – a lot of money at the time because the sport was still growing and the purses going to the drivers (which we paid) were still reasonable.

The people at Valleydale were smart. In their negotiated contract, we were required to sell their hotdogs and chili, which I'm sure enabled them to write the "big check." They also received parking passes, a suite, three hospitality tents and a couple hundred tickets for promotional use, as well as three free color pages of advertising in the event program.

They picked the person to say, "Gentlemen, Start Your Engines!" and they stood alongside me in Victory Lane during the winner's trophy presentation at the end of the race, broadcast live on National TV.

Through the years, some of our sponsors acted like they owned the place. The folks at Valleydale didn't. They were just excited to be involved, but I sensed it would not last for them. It didn't take a mental giant to realize the sport was about to explode – as evidenced by the surge in attendance and TV viewership. Unfortunately, this boom in NASCAR would lead to the demise of participation by most small companies. Bidding wars for sponsorship rights would leave the smaller companies in a cloud of dust. Still, while they were title sponsor, I treated them with as much respect as sponsors from Budweiser, ESPN or Goody's Headache Powders – something Larry demanded.

History can't erase Valleydale from the annals of racing. The 1989 Valleydale Meats 500 won by Rusty Wallace and punctuated by a mêlée of 23 caution flags and 26 wrecks still holds the race records for "most" in both categories at the World's Fastest Half-Mile.

The inevitable came a few weeks after the 1990 Valleydale 500 when company officials from Valleydale announced they would be leaving NASCAR Winston Cup racing. They loved racing. It was just a business decision, nothing personal. So, we now needed an April race event sponsor for the next three years. All of the printing, planning and parties involved made looking for a title sponsorship every year infeasible, just as it would be for a team owner to choose a NASCAR driver every season. Racing relationships are forged over time.

I appreciated the Valleydale folks' honesty as they left the sponsorship and was glad the company continued its presence at the track by ordering a large number of tickets and several hospitality tents. They would be missed in Victory Lane but it was nice to see them still involved.

With Valleydale gone and my lack of experience in luring corporate sponsors into NASCAR racing at the World's Fastest Half-Mile, God apparently felt sorry for me. In a chance meeting with the regional director of the R.J. Reynolds Tobacco Co. (as in the NASCAR Winston Cup series), the discussion turned to our situation without a title sponsor for one of the biggest early events on the spring racing schedule.

As it turned out when I looked at the list of sponsors at other NASCAR tracks – perhaps hoping for divine inspiration – to piggyback on a large company like McDonald's, the Save Mart 500 in California attracted my attention. How in the world could a grocery chain afford to sponsor a NASCAR Winston Cup event?

The answer, I soon learned, was the "mother lode" I was looking for. R.J Reynolds was going to be our new partner. I didn't know it at the time but they were.

Reportedly, Save Mart had a financial partner that was helping pay for its involvement in NASCAR in exchange for prime shelf space in its stores. Made sense to me.

Luckily, Valleydale had informed the track of its decision nearly a year in advance. In talks with Larry Carrier, my attention was consumed with seeking a new title race sponsor.

Ben Beacraft, regional director for R.J. Reynolds at the time, had been a family friend of the Carriers for decades, going back to Larry's founding of Bristol Dragway, on the grounds of Thunder Valley in 1962, and later with his founding of the International Hot Rod Association (IHRA) with Carl Moore.

Beacraft and others met with Carrier and me to discuss their proposal. With the new calculation of the purse and sanctioning fees, the title sponsorship would now cost $125,000 for each of the next three years.

Nearly doubling the fee had me worried. Plus, this early in the talks with "Winston," they weren't just going to pull out their checkbook and write us one for $375,000. And I didn't blame them.

Here was their pitch: We identify a large regional grocery chain that would allow Winston cigarette products to dominate shelf space in all its stores in exchange for the tobacco conglomerate writing the check for the cost of sponsorship and other perks. I actually thought this was a brilliant idea!

"I bet Kroger jumps on this like white on rice," I said in one meeting. Later, I wish I hadn't blurted out that remark since I really didn't know what I was talking about. Still, I thought it was a reasonable proposal and all they could say was, "No." Right?

Much to my surprise, R.J Reynolds' proposal to Kroger landed with a thud. Despite Kroger's then-long history of NASCAR racing involvement, it just wasn't their kind of sponsorship at the time, they said. We have to remember large companies like Kroger, McDonald's, Coca-Cola, etc., get pitched hundreds of times from all over the country seeking their involvement in "great opportunities" from Bristol, Tenn., to Bristol, Conn. (home of ESPN) and even Internationally from here to Bristol, England.

During this period, the federal government was on the verge of banning cigarette advertising, so R.J Reynolds and other tobacco companies were looking for new ways to market their products. I remember in my early days at BIR, Joe Camel would be in the pre-race parade alongside the Planters Peanut Man and other cartoon-like characters – not anymore.

With Kroger out of the picture, Beacraft set his sights on Food City, a company with [at the time] about 30 stores in Northeast Tennessee and Southwest Virginia. I thought he was crazy until I started thinking about the Save Mart 500 in California.

Food City is a family-owned supermarket chain nurtured and founded in 1955 by Jack Smith, who has since passed away. His son, Steve, is now president and CEO. While at the time I questioned Beacraft's selection, if Food City wasn't on board, that only left Food Lion locally, and if both demurred, I was back in line at McDonald's headquarters in Oak Brook, Ill., seeking almost a half-million dollars.

I did know Steve Smith and his dad were huge NASCAR fans and promoters and they always got their associates involved in the racing activities at Bristol and other local tracks. They purchased large blocks of tickets and during race weeks their stores – few in number compared with now – embraced the spirit of NASCAR and the World's Fastest Half-Mile.

Only a few weeks passed, thank God, and a scheduled meeting between, Beacraft, Food City and BIR yielded a pleasant surprise: Food City was in and they signed an agreement to be the title sponsor of the Food City 500 for the next three years. Carrier gave me a cash bonus and a week off with pay.

Not much time passed before I began noticing huge plastic cigarette displays crammed with Winstons, Salems, Cools and Chesterfields brands of cigarette packs at all Food City stores. The colorful red-and-white 6-foot displays were decorated with the familiar Winton Cup Eagle. In cxchange, Food City would enjoy free full sponsorship for the spring Winston Cup series race at Bristol International Raceway. Everyone was happy with this arrangement. I would like to think Food City's involvement with Bristol Raceway enhanced its position in the region where NASCAR race fans are as loyal as family.

Food City has grown from the early years of fewer than 20 stores to the region's supermarket leader with more than 80 locations and counting. The Food City name has also become synonymous with NASCAR racing in the area with its sponsorship of two of the sport's most popular races, the Food City 500 and Food City 300 at Bristol Motor Speedway. As the second longest running sponsor in NASCAR, Food City has also contributed more than a half-million dollars to local organizations through its annual Family Race Night events on State Street in downtown Bristol and in Knoxville, Tenn.

We were always looking for opportunities to market the racetrack and its facilities. We also had the Bristol Sports Arena, located behind Turn 3 where once a month, in the off-season, we promoted professional boxing with "The Budweiser Saturday Night Fight" on ESPN2.

Because we were required to modify the area with a state-of-the art lighting system for TV, the arena was also used during race weeks for the filming of programs like "This Week In NASCAR." Mark Martin looked kind of funny sitting in the boxing ring being interviewed on live TV by Eli Gold. Three hundred tickets were given out to race fans staying in Larry's All American Campground adjacent to the Sports Arena. The television event "This Week In NASCAR" became an annual occurrence that we all looked forward to. Eventually we took the ropes off the ring, and the interview of the driver of the week looked more like he was sitting on a platform rather than a boxing ring.

During one brainstorming session concerning the need to use the track for other events, I pitched to Larry the idea of bringing in top-name entertainment for concerts. Names like Elton John, Guns N' Roses, The Bee Gees and Rod Stewart were tossed around. Larry had, in fact, promoted country concerts at the Bristol Dragway for several years and made a lot of money doing so. Brenda Lee, Alabama, Patsy Cline and other country stars had packed the stands at the Dragway.

I made several trips to Nashville to speak with promoters, including Elton John's representatives. But, at the end of the day, as the Brits are fond of saying, no deals could be reached because – rain or shine – Carrier would be required to guarantee $100,000 up-front booking fee, which was a fortune at the time and a risk that the savvy businessman was not about to take.

In addition, the track was used periodically for national TV commercials and we tried other forms of racing like the All-Pro series. But without the familiar names of NASCAR in those races, they basically bombed. So we concentrated on selling out the races at BIR and developing the World Boxing Federation, as well as our events at the Sports Arena. In fact, that was more than enough to keep us busy.

CHAPTER 7

Carl Moore remembers The Birth of Bristol Motor Speedway

Even though this book deals with my nearly 10 years at BIR, I thought it only fitting to interview Carl Moore, Larry Carrier's track partner from the 1960s. So, in May of 2014 – 53 years after the first checked flag at Bristol International Raceway came down on inaugural race winner Jack Smith – co-founder Carl Moore reflected on the early days at the World's Fastest Half-Mile. At the time Moore and Carrier came up with their plan, I was 5 years old.

"It was actually my idea," Moore says. "I was at a race at Charlotte Motor Speedway and I called Larry [Carrier] who was at his bowling alley, Larry's Lanes, in Bristol. I said, 'Come over here! You gotta see this. There are 50,000 people here who paid $20 a head to see a bunch of race cars going around in a circle.'"

Moore said Carrier locked the door at Larry's Lanes and took the next plane out of Tri-Cities Airport to Charlotte, N.C., where he and Moore watched the Coca-Cola 600.

"When we got back to Bristol, we sat down at a restaurant and put the deal together on the back of a napkin. The next step was to approach Bill France, president of NASCAR, to sanction our race events."

Carrier and Moore had been friends and partners on other business ventures. Moore said he, Larry and the executive vice president of NASCAR met soon thereafter. "We were told to build the track and we'd get the race dates," Moore says. "NASCAR was in its infancy and they were actually looking for more promoters and more facilities in their base, which, at the time, was mostly in the South."

There was just one problem, a big problem. The dynamic duo from Bristol had no money to construct a facility up to NASCAR standards, and, no local bank was interested in taking on a $600,000 project based on a gut feeling that thousands of race fans would come.

"We called Bill France back and explained our circumstances," Moore recalls. "He suggested we talk with the owners of Merlow Vending Machine Co., who managed concessions all over the country and would [probably] be interested in making the loan since they would be getting the track's concession business."

Moore said several meetings were held in New Jersey, where a lot of Scotch was drunk and expensive cigars smoked. "Those party sessions resulted in a final meeting with one of the head men of the company, who said, 'We like you guys and we've decided to make you the loan.'"

However, the risky loan came with a 10 percent interest rate, double at the time what a bank would charge, but Carrier and Moore had no other financial alternative. "The way they dressed and spent money on expensive Scotch, parties, dinners and cigars and drove the best cars had me thinking they had Mafia ties, but I couldn't prove that," Moore adds with a smile.

History tells us that when Bristol International Raceway opened in 1961, it could easily have had a different name and location. The first proposed site for the speedway was in Piney Flats, Tenn., Moore says, a few miles south of the current location.

But, according to Moore, who built the track along with Carrier and construction guru and family friend R.G. Pope, the Piney proposition was not well-received by local residents. "We held a meeting at a Piney Flats church and were on record stating that if anyone was not in favor of the construction and existence of the race track in Piney Flats, [then] we would find another location," Moore says. "Well, several preachers and local citizens did oppose, so, the track that could have been called Piney Flats International Raceway was eventually built on a dairy farm less than 10 miles to the north on Highway 11-E in Bristol.

"One preacher said there would be drinking and gambling and racing on the Lord's Day and he couldn't go along with any of that."

While I was working at BIR, Carrier told me that the track's configuration stemmed from a drawing he commissioned. The drawing depicted a more intimate racetrack setting with a high-banked half-mile facility, rather than what Carrier called a "cookie-cutter 1.5-mile track like Charlotte."

"We didn't have enough land, anyway," Carrier said. "My dad helped us secure the current location."

Construction on Bristol International Speedway began in 1960 and took about a year to finish.

According to Moore, the purchase of the land on which BMS now sits and construction of the track, ate up much of the $600,000 loan. The entire layout for BMS covered 100 acres and provided parking for more than 12,000 cars. The track itself was a perfect half-mile, measuring 60 feet wide on the straightaways and 75 feet wide in the turns, which were banked at 36 degrees.

Seating capacity for the very first NASCAR race at BIR – the Volunteer 500 held on July 30, 1961 – was 18,000, although Carrier said about 7,000 tickets were sold. In November 1970, Carrier and Moore created the International Hot Rod Association and located it behind the "round track." IHRA drew twice the spectators as the NASCAR regular events, because, at the time, drag racing was the racing sport of choice of the ticket-buying public, namely young people.

History shows that when the Volunteer 500 was over, Jack Smith of Spartanburg, S.C., would be forged in the history books as the first winner at BIR. However, Smith wasn't in the driver's seat of the Pontiac when the race ended. He made the first 290 laps but then, with the extreme heat blistering his feet, turned over the duties to Johnny Allen of Atlanta, as his relief driver.

The total purse for the race was $16,625 with the winner's share a whopping $3,225. Forty-two cars started but only 19 finished the bumper-to-bumper event.

"In the early years, the races were not making us any money," Moore says matter-of-factly. "There was no ESPN television money, no Points Fund, and we had to go to the Daytona 500 every year and sign the drivers to compete at Bristol. The biggest stars wanted money for tires, gas and they partied all night long. It was tough signing them because they knew you needed them, especially the big names, to draw a crowd.

"There were no advance sales of race tickets and so ... when we had a rain-out ... you lost your butt. Then, in 1972, when the gas crisis hit, people couldn't or wouldn't travel. That was a devastating time for us!"

Tired of the pressure of having "to go to the bank all the time to borrow money to pay the bills," Moore and Carrier sold out in 1978. Several new owners passed the baton at BIR after going broke. Eventually, when it went into receivership to First American Bank, Carrier regained control of the track, paid all the outstanding debt and received the blessings of NASCAR to return to the helm as owner/general manager of the World's Fastest Half-Mile.

Moore went on to be a highly successful businessman in real estate development and politics, becoming a respected lobbyist and aide to former Tennessee Gov. Ned Ray McWherter. Moore served in the Tennessee General Assembly as both a state representative and state senator. He remains active in business and politics and enjoys raising horses.

Sitting out the 1988 season but helping with boxing events at the Sports Arena, my first race event as the public relations director at Bristol was in April 1989, as "Rusty" Wallace led 174 laps, including the final 101, to win the Valleydale Meats 500. This win was his first Winston Cup victory and the first of nine at Bristol. His success on the high banks is only second to Darrell Waltrip.

The ensuing 10 years would see Carrier allow me to make more big decisions and give me the opportunity to essentially run the company, appointing me vice president and general manager. However, his advice and guidance were always there and he really never gave me complete control, which I surely didn't want. He was one of the smartest racing guys in the world and he pointed me down a path to enjoy the success along with him and his family.

Four years later, I remember vividly how Davey Allison started the 1990s with a bang at Bristol. The 29-year-old son of Bobby and the next generation of the famed Alabama Gang beat Mark Martin by eight inches at the finish line to win the Valleydale Meats 500 on April 8, 1990. The drama did not stop there. When NASCAR returned to Bristol in August, Ernie Irvan, driver of the local, Abingdon, Va.-based Morgan-McClure Motorsports became the third driver to earn his first career win on the high banks. Irvan and Dale Earnhardt led 470 of the 500 laps (with Earnhardt leading 350) but Irvan fought hard in the closing laps to earn the elusive win for MMM.

The win came in front of an estimated crowd of more than 68,000 fans. Carrier had continued with his plans to expand the size of the facility, adding nearly 25,000 seats in the five years since he had re-assumed ownership.

A year after Irvan's dramatic victory, Alan Kulwicki came back from two laps down in the 1991 Bud 500 to earn the first of two consecutive wins at Bristol.

When Kulwicki returned, in April 5, 1992, it marked a couple milestones for the track. First, it was the first Food City 500, a sponsorship that continues today. Secondly, Kulwicki again dominated, winning at Bristol for the second consecutive race. This would be the final race there on an asphalt surface, as well as the last one to be run on bias-ply tires.

The surface and tire changes were spurred by the winning driver himself. In Victory Lane, in front of the members of the press, Kulwicki lambasted me, saying bluntly that the tracked sucked. I still gave him his trophy, but I also called him a son-of-a-bitch. He just smiled.

The increasing traction of the tires was literally eating up the asphalt on the racetrack. Something would need to be done.

—

NASCAR was not the only track on which Carrier and Moore collaborated. They also formed the International Hot Rod Association (IHRA) drag racing sanctioning body in November 1970 that still thrives today. Throughout this period, the organization was operated primarily in the Southeastern United States from its headquarters in Bristol behind the round track where the drag strip was built in 1960. The IHRA initially followed the NHRA's professional class structure of Top Fuel, Funny Car and Pro Stock until the 1984 season when it decided to drop the premier Top Fuel category, an arrangement that only lasted three years before the class was reinstated for the 1987 season.

Carrier is also credited with initiating drag racing's long-term sponsorship association with the R.J. Reynolds Tobacco Company's Winston brand, which ended when the government placed a ban on cigarette advertising. For years, more fans attended events at Bristol Dragway than Bristol International Raceway.

—

Back at the round track, Carrier and I were faced with patching or applying a new coating to the track every couple of races as the increasingly higher speeds combined with the high banks of the track created almost continuous challenges and sleepless nights trying to find ways to keep the racing surface intact and safe.

Our solution was unveiled on Aug. 29, when with the 1992 Budweiser 500, BIR became the first speedway to host a NASCAR Winston Cup event that featured a track surface of all concrete.

Darrell Waltrip led 247 of 500 laps to earn his 12th and final win at Bristol – a record that stands today.

It was only a few years later when, in January 1996, at my urgings and those of his family, Carrier sold Bristol International Raceway to Bruton Smith and Speedway Motorsports Inc., at a purchase price of $26 million "net" with all taxes and attorney fees paid prior to the signing of the deal.

In this 2014 interview, Moore revealed for the first time that he had approached Carrier in 1994 with a $9 million offer from a local group who wanted to move the race dates to another location in Newport, Tenn., where a superspeedway was to be built. Moore said that Carrier, though interested at first, balked at the idea because of his love for Bristol. "He wasn't going along with moving the dates anywhere," Moore said. "So, that squashed the deal."

At the time of the sale, the facility seated about 82,000. Today, Bristol Motor Speedway's capacity is over 160,000, and, a college football game pitting the University of Tennessee Volunteers and the Virginia Tech Hokies is scheduled there on September 10, 2016. In all likelihood, the event will surpass all attendance records for a college football game.

CHAPTER 8

ESPN & BIR – Luck Has It

I became enamored with the business side of racing. I really *did* want to know how track owners like Larry Carrier could garner so much money at the gate from thousands of people who would sit for three hours and watch 42 cars go around in a circle.

Moreover, on top of that revenue, millions could be brought in from television rights, sponsorships and an array of other advertising opportunities offered by racetrack management. For a price, we'll put your name on a wall, in the grass or on a billboard strategically located within the arena.

In 1992, our television contract with ESPN expired. And, with our rating numbers, they of course wanted to renew the television rights for another three years.

I asked Larry why he ever wanted to put a race on television when the idea was to have people come to the track and buy tickets, eat hotdogs and drink beer. "Other track promoters thought I was crazy because at the time the only NASCAR race on TV was the Daytona 500," he said. "I thought, 'Hey, if race fans see the night race on TV with the sparks flying, bumpers banging and tempers flaring, maybe they'll drive to Bristol and see it live and in person.'"

Larry was a visionary. It worked. Soon after the first Bristol race was carried live on ESPN, Bristol International Raceway's NASCAR races were sellouts. In fact, races were selling out a year in advance. You had a better chance of getting a Super Bowl ticket than a ticket to a Bristol race.

And, for ESPN, they enjoyed ratings for Bristol races higher than any other sporting event they carried with the exception of NFL football. So, it was no wonder and a no-brainer that they wanted to renew the television contract.

For those of you who don't know, ESPN's headquarters – ironically – are in Bristol, Conn. It's about 20 miles from Hartford and in the 19th century was known for clock making. Besides being home to ESPN, it is also the home of the oldest theme park still functioning.

January in Bristol, Conn., was not my idea of a good place for the negotiations of our new television contract. Larry hated flying (although in later years, he didn't mind the flight to Las Vegas), so we'd be taking his new Lincoln Navigator wherever the meeting was to be held and I'd be driving as usual.

Since we had to meet, "Let's meet somewhere in the middle if you don't want to come here," suggested ESPN Program Director Rich Caulfield. I began lobbying for New York City, "the city that never sleeps," according to Frank Sinatra. It was also where I had gone to college in the late 1970s and I knew the city well – plenty to do, plenty to see and home to some of the best restaurants in the world. NYC inevitably lost out to Atlantic City.

"It's wintertime and we can stay a few days and play some games," Larry said.

"Gambling games?" I retorted.

"Are there any other kind in Atlantic City?" he asked with a smile.

I've never been much of a gambler. I had been to Las Vegas a couple of times and soon learned they don't build those big hotels and casinos for you to win. Yeah, occasionally someone hits a jackpot. That's why the suckers go back.

Nevertheless, I went to my bank and withdrew $700 of hard-earned money and that was my budget for "playing some games" between meetings with ESPN television executives. I soon discovered three days in a casino hotel is an eternity.

As luck would have it, no pun intended, Larry reached a deal with ESPN over dinner during our first night in Atlantic City. We were staying at Trump Plaza and 20 years ago it was really something to see. It was long before all the "mega" casinos of Las Vegas existed.

Here's the deal on racetrack television contracts. The promoter keeps the TV revenue while he pays NASCAR a hefty sanctioning fee for the rights to the "show." For most NASCAR tracks it represented an important puzzle piece of the financial pie if you expected to make any kind of profit. It also can be dangerous promoting an event outside, because rain or shine, NASCAR collected its sanctioning fee weeks in advance. If you have a rainout, tough luck.

No worriers here. Who cared if it rained, or snowed? We're sold out. Remember? Well, that kind of attitude is also a slap in the face to NASCAR fans and we really never looked at it that way. Winston Cup events, at that time, were preceded by a race in the lower division of NASCAR, called Grand National. Generally speaking, the Grand National division was designed for up-and-coming drivers seeking to gain experience before being elevated to the Big Dance. It was also another revenue stream because many race fans attend both events. What else is there to do while they are in town for the weekend? And, the ticket prices were half of Winston Cup prices, yet in Bristol, many of the "Big Boys" ran in that race too in an attempt to get a jump on the next day's competition.

Grand National races were also shorter, at Bristol, 250 laps as opposed to 500. When you're turning 17-second laps, the race is over before you know it. I spent much of my time promoting the Grand National events because that's what you do when you're sold out!

Back to our meeting in Atlantic City ... Larry was successful in substantially increasing his take for the television rights. ESPN really had no choice because three important items were known by both parties: (1) ESPN knew CBS television executives had approached me about the television rights to Busch 500 night race; (2) At the end of every event we get a report concerning the number of people who watched the race through the Nielsen Television Report that tracks such numbers for sporting events carried on live television, and our number was at the top of the racing list (cable-wise anyway); and (3) ESPN needed reasonably priced events because they were on 24 hours a day 7 days a week and had just announced they would be expanding and adding another network, something called ESPN2, in 1993. Now they would have to develop programs 48 hours a day, 365 days a year.

With the TV rights in hand, ESPN could (and did) broadcast the race as many times as they saw fit. I was experiencing insomnia during a business trip to Canada one time and turned the television on at 3 a.m., and what was on ESPN but a re-broadcast of the Busch 500 NASCAR race from Bristol, Tenn.?

The new three-year ESPN television contract was not only worth hundreds of thousands of dollars more than the previous agreement, but "sly fox" Larry Carrier also walked away with six television dates on the new

ESPN2 television channel for his World Boxing Federation (WBF) professional boxing events at the Bristol Sports Area, located behind the race track.

I still chuckle when recalling that he also convinced Budweiser to be the title sponsor for $10,000 an event, and we were the only boxing arena in the country with a beer sponsor whose product we couldn't even sell!

So, having tucked our copy of the TV contract in my briefcase at 2 a.m., we still had two days left in Atlantic City. The next day, I sat amid hundreds of clanging slot machines amid a bevy of blue-haired ladies who traveled by bus from near and far to the East Coast capital of gambling.

At the end of a long day and night playing dollar slots with Larry, I had managed to only lose about half my money, which I thought was a major accomplishment. After a late-night dinner, it was off to bed at 2 a.m. again only to be roused at 8 a.m. by a knock on the door. When I opened it, I was greeted by a maid, wanting to know if I needed extra towels. I didn't want to be accusatory but the plastic "Do Not Disturb" sign picturing an old man in a bed asleep was nowhere to be found. I took the towels and placed a $5 red poker chip in her outstretched hand and "half-way" slammed the door. When I'm up, I'm up. So, off to the shower I went, at least knowing this would be the last night of the trip and tomorrow night, I'd be sleeping in my own bed on Baxter Street in Johnson City, Tenn.

Later at breakfast, we celebrated taking ESPN – somewhat – to the cleaners. However, they might have been the ones smiling, because we had no clue what they sold the commercials for on the racing broadcast from Bristol. But, we didn't really care. After all, at the end of the day, to make this crazy sport work, all the players have to enjoy the financial rewards of the hard work involved.

It was also a proud day for everyone associated with the track in general and Bristol in particular, because I placed the fifth plaque for "ESPN's Best Track of the Year" on top of the ESPN contract in my briefcase. It's the first time I ordered a T-Bone steak for breakfast.

I shoved my last $1 coin into the machine at 1:30 a.m., actually feeling pretty good that I lasted three days and "only" lost $700. I made the announcement that I was done for the evening. "Hey, Larry I'm beat," I began. "I'm hitting the hay. Long day of driving is ahead. And I have lost my last $1."

"Just stay here until I finish these 'games,' " he said. "It won't be long, the way my luck is going." I spied his machine and he had $112 left. This exercise in $1 machine gambling could take 15 minutes or two hours."

"I don't know, I think I'll just head up to the room. It's no fun just sitting here," I said.

Larry reached for his wallet and pulled out a crisp $100 bill. "So, here. Play some more."

Ok. Why not? I entered the bill into the designated slot and the machine went "bing, bing, bing" until 100 games appeared in the visual plastic counter above it. We were playing dollar machines and the maximum "bet" was $3. Half asleep and disinterested, I punched the counter three times each opportunity and pulled the lever.

Time and time again, I lost. In about 10 minutes, that $100 bill had been reduced to $42. I was so tired that I was literally lying on the machine when, all of a sudden, a red, white and blue 7 appeared across the three panels. Bells and whistles went off and I remarked to Larry, "Hey, look at this. I think I won $300."

Larry peered from over his glasses.

"That's more like $10,000 you lucky [so and so]!"

It wasn't very long before a casino manager made his way to my machine.

"Nice hit," the colorfully dressed man with a red bowtie said.

"Thanks," I oozed like I had just ridden Secretariat to the finish line.

"For security purposes I'm going to ask you to follow me. $10,000 is a lot of money."

"Yes, sir," I responded. "See you in a few, Larry. I'll be back."

In the course of the 10-minute meeting with the casino manager, he gave me information concerning paying taxes on my winnings and asked if they could take my picture for the winners "wall." At this point, I would have Simonized his car.

I, of course, agreed to everything he said. Then came the question I was waiting for.

"Mr. Scalf. How would you like to get paid?"

"Well, sir," I said clearing my throat. "If it's just the same to you, I came in here playing with pictures of dead presidents and I'd like to leave with some of them – if that's OK."

"OK by me. Please fill out this tax form and we'll get your cash. By the way, $10,000 in $100 bills is kinda bulky. Do you have something to put the cash in?"

"Oh yes," I said. "I have a briefcase."

"OK," the nice man answered. "Go get it and we'll fill it up with Ben Franklins," he said with a laugh.

It was funny how the ESPN "Track of the Year" award and the television contract were tossed on the bed, discarded alongside a Tom Clancy novel.

I had to make room for Ben! Beside those items would fit fine in the suitcase compartment along with my dirty socks.

The next morning, we checked out of Trump Plaza and headed back to Bristol, Tenn. I wouldn't return to Atlantic City, N.J., again for years. Larry, Ben and I had a nice trip home. And, I gave Larry his $100 bill back!

CHAPTER 9

Always Building Something

To keep up with the explosive demand for tickets at Bristol International Raceway, it seems like new aluminum seats were added every year from 1986 through 1996. The 1990s did see the sport rapidly expand in popularity, as predicted, and we could have sold as many seats as we wanted to build, and perhaps twice as many, from looking at our massive ticket waiting list. Interestingly, that list included people from all 50 states and nine foreign countries.

When we released a handful of tickets that came available from season ticketholders – because of a death or other unavoidable occurrence – there would be long lines from the front door of the ticket office all the way down Volunteer Parkway. Dozens camped out like we were hosting a rock concert or blockbuster movie premiere, and, unfortunately, most left empty-handed. As a result of the scramble for tickets, scalpers began setting up in makeshift tents along the side of the road from Bristol, Va., to Johnson City, Tenn.

I thought it exceedingly unfair that someone would take advantage of a good thing by gouging our loyal customers, selling our race tickets for twice the face value. Eventually local governments got involved and these self-professed entrepreneurs at least had to purchase "business" permits. This practice continues today, although the spring racing events attract fewer scalpers, since the place now seats more than 150,000 race fans. In addition, the spring NASCAR races are not nearly as popular as the late summer Night Race, which continues to sell out each year.

The popularity of tickets to Bristol races also spilled over into the court system. A local attorney friend told me of a pending divorce in which he was representing the male defendant. A heated debate and controversy erupted as to which party would end up with the Bristol International Raceway tickets. "This screaming debate lasted for weeks," said the lawyer. "My patience was equally growing thin because my fee was only $350 and the debate wasn't worth any more of my time."

"What happened?" I eagerly asked.

"Well, weeks later, we finally reached a compromise," he said. "He gets the spring race tickets one year and she gets the night race tickets and then they flip back and forth each year. I think the funny part of the agreement is a clause that decrees that whoever dies first, the race tickets go to the surviving spouse and/or his/her family.

"From that day forth, I make it a point to inquire whether Bristol race tickets are part of property listed in the divorce petition," he said with a laugh. "I'd been in the middle of trying to work out who got to keep Fido but never race tickets!"

On April 6, 1986, when Rusty Wallace won his first NASCAR Winston Cup race at the Valleydale Meats 500 (He would go on to win eight more.) and after the trophy and "fake check" presentation in Victory Lane, Wallace and I hiked from the infield through the steep stands to the press box for interviews. After three hours in a race car on the most demanding track on the circuit, he was none too happy.

"Ron, this crazy that we have to do this – climb these steps for post-race interviews. If my adrenaline wasn't pumping I'd be pretty f****** upset," he said. "You need to do something about this in the future, 'cause I ain't climbing no more steps, but I do plan on winning more races."

I made a note of the conversation with Rusty, and after talking with Carrier, we installed a state-of-the art sound system so that I could do winner interviews from the Infield Media Center. We then piped the sound up to the press box, a beautiful building with a glass front that sat in Turn 1. If a member of the press in the box wanted a face-to-face interview with the winning driver, he would be the one doing the hiking down to the infield and back. It was the only solution, because you can't put a NASCAR star on a golf cart after he's won the race and drive him through the crowded parking lots up to the press box, located outside the track. At the next Bristol race, I made it a point to tell Rusty we appreciated his suggestion and about our solution. "That's just great Ron," he said with a smile. "You know Bristol is my favorite track!"

"I guess so. It looks like that last win here is goin' to help you win the NASCAR championship this year," I answered.

"Maybe, but it's still August. Lot of racin' left."

In fact, Wallace was crowned the 1986 NASCAR Winston Cup Champion and we forged a 10-year friendship. For several years, he was the track's special guest of honor at the annual Carrier family Christmas celebration at the Bristol Country Club. We counted him as a member of our family and still do.

While we were addressing the problem with press access to the drivers for post-event interviews, Carrier built a building in the infield for Goodyear to store tires, rims and other equipment for test sessions. Previously, tires had to be lugged by hand truck from outside the facility.

And, when a female fan wrote Carrier a letter about the lack of bathroom facilities near the backstretch seats, he built permanent bathroom facilities in that section. We did, however, have dozens of portable toilets placed in the area in which she was sitting. I know. I know. I don't like using those either, but when you have thousands of people at an outdoor event, they are a necessary evil.

More and more seats were added throughout my decade at the racetrack. I learned a valuable lesson from OSHA one day when an inspector made a surprise visit to the track during seat construction and found a worker with a rivet gun – but no hard hat on – high above the track, working on a strand of 6,000 seats. That was a $10,000 "oops." "When money was money," Carrier would say years later, "it was their problem and not ours. The construction company paid the fine because management knew the rules. I always wondered what happened to that guy because I never saw him again."

The fact of the matter is that when one racing weekend concluded, we began the next day preparing for the next racing weekend. More time pressure was on us after the April spring event, because the August race was just around the corner. Our philosophy was to make races the best experience possible for the fans at Bristol International Raceway. "Without them, they wouldn't need us," Carrier was fond of saying.

Many times, we would walk through the grandstands, concession stands, parking lots and souvenir village to gather opinions from our patrons on ways we could make the Bristol experience better.

I remember a conversation with one family (a husband, wife and their two kids) from Wisconsin, who were Alan Kulwicki fans and who suggested we start a shuttle service from our campground located behind Turn 3. "We love Bristol and we come every year, but with two kids, walking from our camper to the front of the track is challenging at best," the mother said. "It's as much a suggestion as a complaint."

So at the next race event, we offered free shuttle service and golf cart rentals throughout the facility to accommodate our customers. We also added souvenir trailers and food vendors to Carrier's All American Campground, which is still in existence today and still owned and managed by the Carrier family. We had a company that would refill your propane tanks, and a man who would drive through the campground selling bags of ice to replenish coolers. Like any business, it's always smart to engage in dialogue with your customers. I can't tell you how many letters of thanks we received from fans.

As the facility grew, the need for additional bathrooms, concession stands, paved parking and ticket booths also grew. The cost was enormous and contracts to perform the improvements always went to local contractors and companies. "We make the money here and we spend it here," Carrier said to his in-house maintenance chief. "There are plenty of people around Bristol who can do this work."

The cost of funding improvements presented a double-edged sword. While wanting to keep ticket prices reasonable, we also did not want to wreck our budget. At the time, Winston Cup tickets at Bristol International Raceway were $65. We never approached the $100 ticket threshold because we felt that was a death knell. It just sounded like too much. A hundred dollars for a race ticket was a lot of money then and now.

We had an excellent yet small maintenance staff whose combined talents could accomplish most any construction project, and they, as a team, saved us a ton of money and enabled us to keep the ticket prices down – and we always sold out.

Along with new fan seating outside came the need for luxury suites inside. The list for suite seating increased after every event. One year, in Turn 4, we built a four-story suite building that was sold out before the first brick was laid. We even sold signage on the front to a local bank for $50,000 and added the cost of a private paved parking lot under the building to the cost of the suite seats. These "packages" were purchased over three-year periods and not one company refused to renew when the time came.

In the campgrounds around the track, including ours, fans began to start coming to the track earlier and earlier as the sport's popularity grew. Hotel rooms from Asheville, N.C., to Knoxville, Tenn., were sold out, so the best alternative was to camp. Campers came in droves. Fans showed up in every make and model camper you can think of for the Bristol experience, and they stayed anywhere from one night to a week. One section of an adjacent campground was called "Tent City." There, hundreds of campers lived in every size and shape tent – from pop-ups to those with generators – all in an effort to enjoy the comforts of outdoor life, only a short walk from the raceway.

Carrier continued to purchase land at the back of the track and convinced the state of Tennessee to improve the roadways for better access. He built a huge shower house for the campers to use free of charge, added tons of gravel for roads and installed guardrail with numbered parking spaces. Throughout the many acres of this former farmland, people from all walks of life would meet, get to know each other and enjoy each other's company. New and lasting friendships were forged.

High on a hill in the All American Campground, a stage with aluminum bleacher seating was constructed for free entertainment for the campers, as well as events such as a McDonald's-hosted breakfast complete with autograph session with their driver at the time, Bill Elliott. Local bands entertained the hundreds of visitors and you didn't have to leave your campsite to hear the music. One time, shortly before his untimely death, we promoted a concert with country star Eddie Rabbit, while toying with the idea of hosting country music events at the campground.

In 1993, a souvenir store was built, offering merchandise year-round. Every popular NASCAR driver had his own shelf space and the store was an instant hit, especially around Christmas.

Advertising billboards located inside the track were constructed, painted and installed by track employees. A crane was sometimes needed for placement, and the track's banking made placement a challenge. Still, all the space available inside the track remained sold during my decade there. Because of the weather, however, every billboard had to be repainted and refurbished nearly every year.

For a fee you could buy space on a fence or near the hospitality village to hang a banner. Normally, these banners were gone after the event and are probably hanging in garages and party rooms across the country.

For some of the race fans camping behind the track, food concessions and ice vendors became our partners. You could buy ice wholesale for 75 cents a bag and we sold a bag for $1. On a hot August day, we probably could have sold a bag for $3 but we weren't in the "ripping people off" game.

One of the most interesting construction projects in Carrier's All American Campground was the conversion of a small opened-faced block building at the front of the campground from cover for Coke machines into a diner. We were approached by local entrepreneur Brad

Cook, who said, "I want to rent that little building and turn it in to a small restaurant ... selling hamburgers, hot dogs, breakfast sandwiches, etc."

Next thing I knew, Cook had done just that, complete with picnic tables in front and music to draw a crowd. Space was at a premium and Brad and his wife turned a Coke machine plaza into a fan's favorite stop, especially those sleeping in tents with no way to cook food.

To keep up with the year-round popularity of NASCAR, we constructed a souvenir shop at the entrance to the track. Carrier also petitioned Steak & Shake, his favorite on-the-road hamburger chain, to come to Bristol and build a restaurant adjacent the souvenir shop. It surprised me that Carrier was turned down. A study was made of "roof tops" (population numbers) in the community, leading Steak & Shake management to decline the offer, saying the store wouldn't be profitable year-round. Two race weekends did not equate to the steady numbers the franchise needed.

Carrier didn't mind spending money on the facility when it was warranted. The track's maintenance shop was small and cramped and left little storage room. At the urging of his maintenance chief, he built a state-of-the art maintenance building and purchased enough equipment to address any problem or building project.

For years, if you camped in the campground, you would have to drive several miles from the campgrounds to the front of the track. So, as the crowds became larger and the campgrounds sold out of space, Carrier petitioned the state for the right to build a bridge at his cost across Beaver Creek so that fans could walk the short distance to the track. The concrete access bridge is still being used today.

CHAPTER 10

Food City Race Night & other celebrations

Mike Snapp knows all about Food City Race Night. After all, he probably started it in 1987 without really realizing it. He was working for Stuart Wood, owner of the local Budweiser distributorship in Johnson City, Tenn., 17 miles south of the racetrack.

As race sponsor of the Budweiser 250 and the Bud 500, Snapp was involved with scheduling Budweiser's driver appearances along with legendary car owner and former NASCAR Champion Junior Johnson, in conjunction with promoting Eagle Snacks, and Anheuser Busch beer products.

As chain account manager, Snapp also scheduled appearances by the ever-popular Bud Girls and the Budweiser show car at Tri-Cities supermarkets and convenience stores.

"Stuart basically would take Junior Johnson and whoever the driver was that year along with Ned Jarrett, Busch beer spokesman [also a famous former NASCAR champion and father to Dale Jarrett, another NASCAR champ in his own right] to Skoby's Restaurant in Kingsport or Salt Water Willy's," Snapp recalls. "I would say, 'Oh, by the way, can you swing by Food City on Eastman Road and sign a few autographs?' Basically he would agree.

"Ed Moore and Tom Embrey, at Food City, were friends, as well as our partners in the beer business. They never knew that I didn't know at the time whether the group along with race car driver Terry Labonte would show up or not! So unbeknownst to me, Moore calls the local radio station, and the next thing I know, there is a live remote in the parking lot and the station is telling people there will be an autograph session at this particular Food City. I looked around about an hour later and there were over 2,000 people in the parking lot and in the store, and shopping had come to a grinding halt. I had a time in my mind when they should arrive after eating supper but that time passed and the clock was ticking.

" 'Where are they?' a frantic Embrey asked. 'I don't know,' I said. 'What do you mean you don't know? You mean to tell me you don't know if they are coming here to sign autographs or not?' 'No, but I think they are,' I answered."

Snapp says he was sweating and pacing, and, by this time, there were 1,000 cars in the parking lot. "It was calm madness ... if there is such a thing," Snapp says. "I was just thinking, 'When, where, when, where are they?' And I was thinking about all the bad things that were going to happen to me over this one."

Just when the suspense climaxed and someone was going to have to tell the crowd that the NASCAR stars would not be making an appearance, a van pulled up in front of the store and a smiling and waving Junior Johnson hopped out followed by Terry Labonte, Ned Jarrett and Stuart Wood.

Food City Race Night & other celebrations

"The crowd goes wild!" Snapp says. "I can laugh about it now but I still remember the sick feeling I had that night. We had built these massive beer displays where they would be separated from the fans but the fans could get their autographs. Turns out, [the racing celebrities] loved every minute of it and they signed autographs for over an hour. I guess I was a hero because it worked, but if it hadn't, I would have probably been without a job, or at least Budweiser would have lost shelf space in Food City stores."

Snapp says that the next year, he made the same request with similar results. Food City managers offered free samples and added games inside the stores, such as Turkey Bowling where customers rolled a frozen 10-pound turkey down an aisle to win prizes depending on how many plastic pins they knocked down.

The event was so popular that the word got out in the retail industry, and Snapp says success breeds success. "Tide wanted in. This store brand wanted in. That store brand wanted in," Snapp says with a smile. "It had gotten so big 'Race Night' was then moved the next year to J. Fred Johnson Stadium [high school football facility in Kingsport] where drivers were placed in individual tents to sign autographs. And, that was the end of the Food City appearance by our driver and support team and the birth of Food City Race Night."

Always held in August, the Thursday prior to the Night Race at Bristol Motor Speedway, the cities of Bristol, Tenn., and Bristol, Va., close downtown streets for the celebration. Drivers sign autographs along State Street, which is shared by both states, and there are food vendors and entertainment aplenty. The event draws 30,000 people to the Bristols' downtown every year.

Today, there is not a bigger, more successful event than Food City Race Night for race fans in conjunction with NASCAR anywhere in America.

Reflecting more on his involvement with Budweiser and Bristol International Raceway, Snapp says the sport and track have changed from the "good old days."

"When we started dealing with people at the track who were wearing loafers with no socks, I knew the track was changing," Snapp says. "And, when we got out [locally] and Budweiser corporate took over, the family track turned into the corporate track. I remember asking myself, 'What's happening here?' "

Snapp has fond memories of bringing the Budweiser Clydesdales horses to the track for the first time and safely sliding down the high banks in a six-bay truck to bring beer into the infield, to the drivers and their guests on a snowy race weekend. He also had the pleasure of being the "Official Starter" at one of the Budweiser 250 races.

He also shares a funny story about bringing to BIR a Toyota van – before Toyota's involvement in NASCAR – that was decorated like a race car with logos and stickers from race sponsors. The van basically was used as another "show car" to promote NASCAR racing and, of course, Budweiser.

"I drove it into the pits and left it there until the race was over," he says. "It was the only vehicle there that was not American made. No one let me out and I was the last to leave the track at 2 a.m."

"Racin' the way it was?" I ask with a laugh.

"Yep, those were good times and it was racing the way it was," Snapp agrees.

CHAPTER 11

Concrete replaces asphalt at BIR and Carrier shocks the racing world

As NASCAR Winston Cup racing moved into the 1990s, so did brand new state-of-the art automobile technology. The aerodynamics of stock cars had them flying around Bristol International Raceway at breakneck speeds. Records for the pole position seemed to be shattered at every event. When Mark Martin set the track record of 120.278 mph for the pole position at the 1989 Valleydale Meats 500, cars were finishing a lap in an amazing 17 seconds – unless, of course, a driver got caught up in a wreck ... a frequent occurrence.

With BIR's 38-degree, steep banking and the speeds of 36 3,000-pound racecars slingshotting and pushing hard into the four corners, this was a formula for disaster for the racetrack's asphalt surface.

Following the 1991 running of the Food City 500 on April 9, a routine day-after inspection of the racing surface revealed a horrifying fact. The track was literally coming apart in the corners!

Carrier had little choice but to repave the track at a cost that would run into nearly a half million dollars. I remember thinking I wish I'd gotten more money from Winston and Food City.

"We have no choice but to get on the paving project right now," Carrier said. "We have to give the surface time to cure for the August night race [Goody's 500]. I may be sick about it but whatayou going to do?" To make matters worse, underneath Turn 4 is a French drain that collects runoff water from the 36-degree banking. You just don't mess with stuff like that, I thought.

Paving just the corners of the track was a great idea I proposed to Carrier to save money. "Won't work," Carrier said. "I'm paving it all. Might as well why we're at it. It'll be new and uniform. The drivers expect it, NASCAR expects it and the fans deserve it."

So let the paving begin!

Adamant about putting local people to work, Carrier, a former award-winning housing subdivision builder, hired a local paving company to tear up the old asphalt and replace it with a new piping hot mixture. They began in mid-April and were finished in mid-May, well enough time for the August night race, the most popular NASCAR race as voted by the fans. On the high banks of BIR, cranes held the paving machines in place. It was a breath-taking sight. I turned down all media requests until the day it was finished. Then we called a press conference in the press box overlooking this crown jewel. The infield walls, Victory Lane and support buildings had been repainted and new striping had been added just for the occasion. The Winston Cup Eagle looked event redder and NASCAR's logo was emblazoned everywhere, signifying a job well done. Even the U.S. and Tennessee flags welcomed the early summer breeze.

Filling reporters' bellies in advance of the tour of the new surface seemed like a good idea, although there was little about the resurfacing to criticize. The news media was more than kind, which is a far cry from some of the reactions from drivers who ran in the last race before the repairs. If you want a good case of ulcers, have a racing event stopped because your track is coming up.

The spring and summer seasons of 1991 seemed to pass faster than normal and, before I knew it, the Busch 500 Night Race weekend was upon us. Because we wanted the track to cure for as long as possible, we – with NASCAR's blessing – allowed only minimum testing by single-car teams, and up to the day of the Truck Race, there had been no issues.

The usual parties and Food City Race Night welcomed fans to the most popular race weekend on the NASCAR Winston Cup schedule. The sold-out Night Race at Bristol was complemented by the Food City 250 and NASCAR Camping World Truck race the night before. To say there was apprehension in the offices at the track would be an understatement. We hoped the track would hold and the usual beating and banging from 36 race cars under the lights would result in yet another memorable weekend.

Fortunately, the running of the Food City 250 Busch Grand National and the Truck Race would occur the night before, to gauge any significant surface problems. Midway through the Truck Race, there were some assault pebbles mixed with tire rubber, but that was not atypical on the previous surface. With each passing lap, the heavy trucks took a toll on the corners and Turn 4 lost its grip.

Team owner Richard Childress and others met Carrier and me on the track where a chunk of asphalt had broken loose. Luckily, the event was nearly finished and patch work to Turn 3 held until the next night when the Food City 250 NASCAR Busch Grand National race was run.

The same thing happened as the previous night except this time, both turns 1 and 4 starting coming up. The race was red flagged until we were able to patch the holes using, this time, a concrete mixture.

After handing the winner's trophy to Dale Jarrett, I headed to the infield media center for the after-race press conference knowing that I'd not sleep well that night.

The following night was a nervous one for the BIR staff.

The pageantry of the summer Saturday night race on the high banks of Bristol is unlike anything else in motorsports. Trying to reproduce this unique spectacle would be like trying to duplicate the Eiffel Tower or repaint a Mona Lisa, and that ain't happening. The weeklong schedule of events, parties and cookouts had all concluded, and with high anticipation, I stepped to the microphone and welcomed the thousands of fans into the last great coliseum, once compared to flying jet airplanes in a gymnasium.

As each 17-second lap clicked by, thoughts and prayers were for the track to remain intact giving us eight months for it to cure before the spring event. I soon learned lighter Busch cars and 250 laps spaced between stops and starts for wrecks and cautions was little comparison to what unfolded that hot August night in Bristol, Tenn.

By lap 124, the asphalt surface in Turn 4 began to break loose again because the race cars were pushing into the corner at such high speeds. The caution flag flew for what I originally thought was debris on the track caused by a wreck three laps earlier. A sick feeling hit my stomach when NASCAR officials summoned Larry and me again to the infield media center for a firsthand inspection of the surface problem.

We limped out of our 1991 season with some major track surface issues, but the good news was that we had eight months to figure out the problem, in time for the 1992 Food City 500. Carrier knew he could ill-afford to pave the track every year. It just wasn't a financially viable option.

After each race weekend concludes, the staff takes a hiatus to recover from the stress of living in a vacuum for the preceding three months, preparing for the event.

Since we were the most popular track on the circuit, we weren't worried (as some venues were) about starting the following day selling tickets for the next event. In fact, the 1992 NASCAR Winston Cup races were sold out by the time the checkered flag dropped on the race the night before.

While the others were recuperating, Carrier and I were in his office at 11 a.m. the following day to assess his plan for dealing with the track for the next race. He had not slept, and neither had I.

UNOFFICIAL RESULTS OF THE BUD 500 WINSTON CUP SERIES RACE, BIR, AUGUST 24, 1991

Finishing Position	Starting Position	Car Number	Driver	Team/Car	Laps	Money	Reason Out
1	5	7	Alan Kulwicki	Hooters Ford	500	$61,400	Running
2	14	22	Sterling Marlin	Maxwell House Ford	500	$30,275	Running
3	27	25	Ken Schrader	Kodiak Chevrolet	500	$22,950	Running
4	10	6	Mark Martin	Folgers Ford	499	$19,700	Running
5	17	5	Ricky Rudd	Tide Chevrolet	499	$16,450	Running
6	18	15	Morgan Shepherd	Motorcraft Ford	498	$13,125	Running
7	13	3	Dale Earnhardt	GM Goodwrench Chevrolet	498	$16,025	Running
8	3	17	Darrell Waltrip	Western Auto Chevrolet	498	$9,275	Running
9	28	94	Terry Labonte	Sunoco Oldsmobile	493	$9,225	Running
10	32	26	Brett Bodine	Quaker State Buick	493	$11,875	Running
11	23	66	Lake Speed	TropArtic Pontiac	492	$8,425	Running
12	30	43	Richard Petty	STP Pontiac	491	$8,125	Running
13	6	68	Bobby Hamilton	Country Time Oldsmobile	490	$7,125	Running
14	4	19	Chad Little	Bulls Eye Ford	489	$5,025	Running
15	11	98	Jimmy Spencer	Banquet Frozen Foods Chevrolet	489	$20,375	Running
16	19	55	Ted Musgrave	Grindstaff Jaspar Pontiac	488	$5,925	Running
17	24	75	Joe Ruttman	Dinner Bell Foods Oldsmobile	483	$6,975	Running
18	26	4	Ernie Irvan	Kodak Chevrolet	449	$10,775	Running

19	25	33	Harry Gant	Skoal Bandit Oldsmobile	436	$6,865	Running
20	12	8	Rick Wilson	Snickers Buick	409	$7,750	Engine Failure
21	1	9	Bill Elliott	Coors Light Ford	404	$13,575	Running
22	9	12	Hut Stricklin	Raybestos Brakes Buick	403	$6,450	Running
23	22	71	Dave Marcis	Big Apple Market Chevrolet	400	$6,375	Running
24	7	28	Davey Allison	Texaco Havoline Ford	377	$11,550	Engine Failure
25	31	30	Michael Waltrip	Pennzoil Pontiac	350	$6,205	Running
26	8	1	Rick Mast	Skoal Classic Oldsmobile	344	$5,575	Engine Failure
27	21	24	Dick Trickle	Team III Pontiac	313	$4,050	Accident
28	16	21	Dale Jarrett	Citgo Ford	253	$5,500	Accident
29	20	10	Derrick Cope	Purolator Chevrolet	239	$11,075	Engine Failure
30	15	42	Bobby Hillin	Mello Yello Pontiac	220	$9,625	Running
31	29	11	Geoff Bodine	Budweiser Ford	183	$11,425	Accident
32	2	2	Rusty Wallace	Miller Genuine Draft Pontiac	88	$4,425	Handling

Time of Race: 3 hours, 14 minutes, 56 seconds
Average Speed: 82.028 mph
Margin of Victory: 9.4 seconds
Caution Flags: 11 for 80 laps
Lead Changes: 11 lead changes among 8 drivers
Attendance: 60,500

UNOFFICIAL RESULTS OF THE 32ND ANNUAL BUD 500 NASCAR WINSTON CUP RACE
BRISTOL INTERNATIONAL RACEWAY, BRISTOL, TN , SATURDAY, AUGUST 29, 1992

Finishing Position	Starting Position	Car Number	Driver	Team/Car	Laps	Money	Running or Reason Out
1	9	17	Darrell Waltrip	Western Auto Chevrolet	500	$73,050	Running
2	23	3	Dale Earnhardt	GM Goodwrench Chevrolet	500	$39,325	Running
3	6	25	Ken Schrader	Kodiak Chevrolet	500	$28,350	Running
4	26	42	Kyle Petty	Mello Yello Pontiac	500	$18,000	Running
5	5	7	Alan Kulwicki	Hooters Ford	499	$19,800	Running
6	19	11	Bill Elliott	Budweiser Ford	499	$18,075	Running
7	12	66	Jimmy Hensley	TropArtic Ford	499	$11,775	Running
8	2	5	Ricky Rudd	Tide/Exxon Chevrolet	499	$16,875	Running
9	3	26	Brett Bodine	Quaker State Ford	499	$14,225	Running
10	8	2	Rusty Wallace	Miller Genuine Draft Pontiac	498	$14,575	Running
11	11	15	Geoff Bodine	Motorcraft Ford	497	$14,425	Running
12	17	10	Derrike Cope	Purolator Chevrolet	497	$9,115	Running
13	15	21	Morgan Shepherd	Cirgo Ford	497	$11,775	Running
14	22	30	Michael Waltrip	Pennzoil Pontiac	497	$11,525	Running
15	27	22	Sterling Marlin	Maxwell House Ford	495	$11,325	Running
16	30	43	Richard Petty	STP Pontiac	493	$10,775	Running
17	14	18	Dale Jarrett	Interstate Batteries Chevrolet	492	$10,525	Running
18	31	71	Jim Sauter	Marcis Racing Chevrolet	491	$7,375	Running

19	21	16	Wally Dallenbach	Keystone Beer Ford	489	$5,465	Running
20	29	20	Jimmy Spencer	Food City Ford	487	$6,125	Running
21	28	68	Bobby Hamilton	Country Time Oldsmobile	484	$11,075	Running
22	25	55	Ted Musgrave	Jasper Engines Ford	476	$9,925	Running
23	10	8	Dick Trickle	Snickers Ford	446	$6,775	Running
24	32	52	Jimmy Means	Taco Bell Pontiac	395	$6,650	Running
25	4	6	Mark Martin	Valvoline Ford	385	$13,605	Accident
26	16	33	Harry Gant	Skoal Bandit Oldsmobile	349	$15,475	Accident
27	13	12	Hut Stricklin	Raybestos Chevrolet	339	$9,525	Engine
28	1	4	Ernie Irvan	Kodak Chevrolet	285	$17,000	Handling
29	24	1	Rick Mast	Skoal Classic Oldsmobile	274	$9,425	Accident
30	7	28	Davey Allison	Texaco Ford	262	$16,025	Accident
31	18	94	Terry Labonte	Sunoco Ultra Oldsmobile	125	$9,350	Engine
32	20	41	Dave Marcis	Kellogg's Chevrolet	101	$6,325	Accident

Time of Race: 2 hours, 55 minutes, 20 seconds
Average Speed: 91.198 mph
Margin of Victory: 9.28 seconds
Lead Changes: 14 among 8 drivers
Caution Flags: 10 for 55 laps
Estimated Attendance: 64,870 BRISTOL TRACK RECORD

UNOFFICIAL FINAL RESULTS OF THE BUD 500—NASCAR WINSTON CUP RACE
BRISTOL INTERNATIONAL RACEWAY, BRISTOL, TN, AUGUST 28, 1993

Finishing Position	Starting Position	Car Number	Driver	Team/Car	Laps	Money	Running or Reason Out
1	1	6	Mark Martin	Valvoline Ford	500	$80,125	Running
2	2	2	Rusty Wallace	Miller Genuine Draft Pontiac	500	$31,875	Running
3	19	3	Dale Earnhardt	GM Goodwrench Chevrolet	500	$32,325	Running
4	10	33	Harry Gant	Skoal Bandit Chevrolet	500	$28,150	Running
5	12	1	Rick Mast	Skoal Classic Ford	500	$22,000	Running
6	9	7	Jimmy Hensley	Family Channel Ford	500	$12,075	Running
7	13	26	Brett Bodine	Quaker State Ford	500	$16,925	Running
8	11	15	Geoff Bodine	Motorcraft Ford	500	$18,925	Running
9	23	40	Kenny Wallace	Dirt Devil Pontiac	499	$12,600	Running
10	24	30	Michael Waltrip	Pennzoil Pontiac	498	$17,600	Running
11	14	11	Bill Elliott	Budweiser Ford	498	$19,300	Running
12	31	90	Bobby Hillin	Hellig-Meyers Ford	497	$8,900	Running
13	16	21	Morgan Shepherd	Citgo Ford	497	$14,550	Running
14	25	41	Phil Parsons	Manheim Auto Auctions Chevrolet	497	$11,300	Running
15	4	22	Bobby Labonte	Maxwell House Coffee Ford	495	$12,500	Running
16	21	28	Lake Speed	Texaco Havoline Ford	493	$18,350	Running
17	29	71	Dave Marcis	Tri-City Aviation	484	$8,300	Running

				Chevrolet			
18	27	52	Jimmy Means	NAPA Ford	483	$8,250	Running
19	28	68	Greg Sacks	Country Time Ford	483	$8,240	Running
20	8	24	Jeff Gordon	DuPont Chevrolet	466	$11,450	Running
21	22	16	Wally Dallenback	Keystone Beer Ford	437	$13,000	Running
22	3	5	Ricky Rudd	Tide Chevrolet	414	$13,900	Running
23	30	8	Sterling Marlin	Raybestos Ford	374	$12,750	Running
24	26	25	Ken Schrader	Kodiak Chevrolet	354	$12,575	Running
25	32	12	Jimmy Spencer	Meineke Ford	325	$12,430	Running
26	34	4	Ernie Irvan	Kodak Film Chevrolet	316	$17,650	Engine Fail
27	7	98	Derrike Cope	Bojangles Ford	292	$12,325	Transmission
28	6	44	Rick Wilson	STP Pontiac	274	$9,250	Engine Fail
29	17	17	Darrell Waltrip	Western Auto Chevrolet	246	$17,450	Running
30	20	42	Kyle Petty	Mello Yello Pontiac	207	$16,600	Accident
31	33	18	Dale Jarrett	Interstate Batteries Chevrolet	199	$17,450	Running
32	5	27	Hut Stricklin	McDonald's Ford	83	$12,150	Accident
33	15	20	Bobby Hamilton	Fina Lube Ford	30	$15,600	Rear End
34	18	14	Terry Labonte	Kellogg's Chevrolet	30	$12,125	Accident

Time of Race: 3 hours, 1 minute, and 21 seconds
Average Speed: 88.172 mph
Margin of Victory: 1 car length
Lead Changes: 8 among 4 drivers
Caution flags: 11 for 71 laps
Estimated attendance: 72500 (RECORD)

NASCAR WINSTON CUP RACE NUMBER 20—1989 SEASON
BUSCH 500—BRISTOL INTERNATIONAL RACEWAY
Bristol, Tennessee--.533 Mile Paved Speedway
August 26, 1989—266.5 M—500 L—Purse: $413,792

Finishing Position	Starting Position	Car Number	Driver	Team	Laps	Winston Cup Points	Bonus Points	Total Money Won	Reason Out of Race
1	9	17	Darrell Waltrip	Tide Chevrolet	500	185	10	$52,450	
2	1	7	Alan Kulwicki	Zerex Ford	500	175	5	$30,875	
3	6	26	Ricky Rudd	Quaker State Buick	500	165		$19,200	
4	14	33	Harry Gant	Skoal Bandit Oldsmobile	500	160		$13,300	
5	16	11	Terry Labonte	Budweiser Ford	499	155		$13,400	
6	10	27	Rusty Wallace	Kodiak Pontiac	499	155	5	$12,125	
7	24	8	Bobby Hillin	Miller High Life Buick	498	146		$7,800	
8	12	88	Jimmy Spencer	Crisco Pontiac	496	142		$7,900	
9	31	21	Neil Bonnett	Citgo Ford	495	138		$9,307	
10	30	29	Dale Jarrett	Hardee's Pontiac	494	134		$10,975	
11	17	55	Phil Parsons	Crown Oldsmobile	493	127		$6,100	
12	28	71	Dave Marcis	Lifebuoy Soap Chevrolet	492	124		$5,900	
13	13	66	Rick Mast	Food City Chevrolet	492	124		$3,150	
14	7	3	Dale Earnhardt	GM Goodwrench Chevrolet	490	126	5	$11,650	
15	8	2	Ernie Irvan	Kroger Pontiac	489	118		$4,750	
16	2	5	Geoff Bodine	Levi Garrett Chevrolet	488	120	5	$8,850	
17	3	15	Brett Bodine	Motorcraft Ford	488	112		$5,525	
18	5	94	Sterling Marlin	Sunoco Oldsmobile	464	109		$4,950	
19	32	57	Hut Stricklin	Heinz Pontiac	463	106		$3,250	

20	23	6	Mark Martin	Stroh's Light Ford	458	103		$5,500	
21	19	16	Larry Pearson	Chattanooga Chew Buick	444	100		$3,025	Overheating
22	27	42	Kyle Petty	PEAK Pontiac	322	97		$2,250	Accident
23	4	25	Ken Schrader	Folger's Coffee Chevrolet	294	94		$7,295	Engine Failure
24	21	9	Bill Elliott	Coors Ford	246	91		$11,190	Engine Failure
25	20	28	Davey Allison	Havoline Ford	241	88		$8,935	Running
26	29	75	Morgan Shepherd	Valvoline Pontiac	223	85		$8,680	Engine Failure
27	18	4	Rick Wilson	Kodak Film Oldsmobile	142	82		$4,350	Engine Failure
28	22	84	Dick Trickle	Miller High Life Buick	126	79		$4,300	Accident
29	15	10	Derrike Cope	Purolator Pontiac	121	76		$2,725	Accident
30	26	48	Greg Sacks	Dinner Bell Pontiac	59	PE		$2,600	Engine Failure
31	25	83	Joe Ruttman	Bull's Eye Barbecue Sauce Oldsmobile	57	PE		$3,600	Accident
32	11	30	Michael Waltrip	Country Time Lemonade Pontiac	57	67		$4,100	Accident

Time of Race: 3 hours, 4 minutes, 14 seconds
Average Speed: 85.554 MPH
Margin of Victory: 5.04 seconds
Busch Pole Award: Alan Kulwicki, Zerex Ford, 117.043 mph (16.394 seconds)
Busch Fastest Second-Round Qualifier: Greg Sacks, Dinner Bell Pontiac
True Value Hard Charger Award: Darrell Waltrip, Tide Chevrolet (Kulwicki, Earnhardt, Labonte, G. Bodine)
Van Camp's Determination Award: Dale Jarrett, Hardee's Pontiac (Dave Marcis)
TRW Mechanic of the Race: Jeff Hammond, Tide Chevrolet
Goody's Headache Award: Dale Earnhardt, GM Goodwrench Chevrolet
Dinner Bell Top Dog Award: Darrell Waltrip, Tide Chevrolet
Heinz Ketchup Award Winner: Neil Bonnett, Citgo Ford
Caution Flags: 11 for 69 laps (60-64, 92-94, 98-100, 105-109, 130-136, 199-202, 205-227, 298-302, 315-317, 325-332, 375-377)

UNOFFICIAL RESULTS OF THE FOOD CITY 500 WINSTON CUP SERIES RACE
BRISTOL INTERNATIONAL RACEWAY—BRISTOL, TN—APRIL 5, 1992

Finishing Position	Starting Position	Car Number	Driver	Team/Car	Laps	Money	Reason Out
1	1	7	Alan Kulwicki	Hooter's Ford	500	$83,360	Running
2	4	18	Dale Jarrett	Interstate Batteries Chevrolet	500	$29,835	Running
3	8	25	Ken Schrader	Kodiak Chevrolet	500	$29,410	Running
4	15	94	Terry Labonte	Sunoco Ultra Oldsmobile	499	$20,010	Running
5	22	8	Dick Trickle	SNICKERS Ford	499	$18,410	Running
6	17	5	Ricky Rudd	Tide Chevrolet	497	$16,485	Running
7	13	21	Morgan Shepherd	Citgo Ford	496	$13,685	Running
8	5	12	Hut Stricklin	Raybestos Brakes Chevrolet	495	$13,185	Running
9	3	2	Rusty Wallace	Miller Genuine Draft Pontiac	494	$15,280	Running
10	31	10	Derrike Cope	Purolator Chevrolet	494	$15,280	Running
11	2	26	Brett Bodine	Quaker State Ford	494	$12,680	Running
12	27	15	Geoff Bodine	Motorcraft Ford	494	$11.730	Running
13	29	41	Greg Sacks	Kellogg's Chevrolet	492	$6,055	Running
14	24	55	Ted Musgrave	Jasper Engines Oldsmobile	492	$11,105	Running
15	9	6	Mark Martin	Valvoline Ford	488	$13,905	Running
16	25	9	Dave Mader III	Food City Ford	487	$11,430	Running
17	10	30	Michael Waltrip	Pennzoil Pontiac	478	$10,530	Running
18	18	3	Dale Earnhardt	GM Goodwrench Chevrolet	471	$18,130	Running

19	23	42	Kyle Petty	Mello Yello Pontiac	471	$10,420	Running
20	11	11	Bill Elliott	Budweiser Ford	470	$14,230	Running
21	26	52	Brad Teague	Stock Car Min. Pontiac	456	$7,080	Running
22	32	16	Wally Dallenbach	Keystone Pontiac	446	$5,280	Running
23	20	66	Chad Little	TropArtic Ford	439	$4,880	Running
24	7	4	Ernie Irvan	Kodak Chevrolet	415	$14,755	Accident
25	16	17	Darrell Waltrip	Western Auto Chevrolet	382	$24,505	Running
26	28	68	Bobby Hamilton	Country Time Oldsmobile	379	$10,680	Running
27	14	43	Richard Petty	STP Pontiac	354	$9,630	Running
28	6	28	Davey Allison	Havoline-Texaco Ford	335	$15,205	Running
29	12	33	Harry Gant	Skoal Oldsmobile	277	$14,975	Engine
30	30	1	Rick Mast	Skoal Classic Oldsmobile	122	$9,480	Accident
31	21	71	Dave Marcis	Big Apple Market Chevrolet	92	$6,455	Engine
32	19	22	Sterling Marlin	Maxwell House Coffee Ford	16	$9,430	Accident

Time of Race: 3 hours, 5 minutes, 15 seconds
Average Speed: 86.316 mph
Margin of Victory: .78 seconds
Caution Flags: 10 for 75 laps
Leader changes: 11 lead changes among 7 drivers
Attendance: 62,300

UNOFFICIAL RESULTS OF THE FOOD CITY 500 NASCAR WINSTON CUP RACE
BRISTOL INTERNATIONAL RACEWAY, BRISTOL, TN, SUNDAY, APRIL 4, 1993

Finishing Position	Starting Position	Car Number	Driver	Team	Laps	Money	Running or Reason Out
1	1	2	Rusty Wallace	Miller Genuine Draft Pontiac	500	$107,610	Running
2	6	3	Dale Earnhardt	GM Goodwrench Chevrolet	500	$47,760	Running
3	14	42	Kyle Petty	Mello Yello Pontiac	500	$31,485	Running
4	28	12	Jimmy Spencer	Meineke Mufflers Ford	500	$26,050	Running
5	10	28	Davey Allison	Texaco Havoline Ford	500	$25,180	Running
6	35	17	Darrell Waltrip	Western Auto Chevrolet	500	$23,405	Running
7	4	21	Morgan Shepherd	Citgo Ford	499	$17,305	Running
8	8	6	Mark Martin	Valvoline Ford	498	$19,055	Running
9	2	26	Brett Bodine	Quaker State Ford	497	$16,150	Running
10	19	1	Rick Mast	Skoal Classic Ford	497	$17,650	Running
11	25	16	Wally Dallenbach Jr.	Keystone Beer Ford	496	$14,950	Running
12	12	98	Derrike Cope	Bojangles' Ford	494	$15,500	Running
13	30	40	Kenny Wallace	Dirt Devil Pontiac	494	$9,825	Running
14	15	30	Michael Waltrip	Pennzoil Pontiac	492	$13,875	Running
15	32	55	Ted Musgrave	Jasper Engines Ford	488	$13,825	Accident
16	31	52	Jimmy Means	NAPA Ford	484	$8,450	Running
17	21	24	Jeff Gordon	DuPont Chevrolet	481	$9,400	Accident

18	5	15	Geoff Bodine	Motorcraft Ford	469	$16,350	Running
19	27	20	Joe Ruttman	Finalube Ford	467	$8,340	Running
20	17	8	Sterling Marlin	Raybestos Ford	443	$13,200	Running
21	18	14	Terry Labonte	Kellogg's Chevrolet	440	$12,950	Running
22	34	75	Dick Trickle	Carolina Pottery Ford	440	$8,050	Running
23	3	4	Ernie Irvan	Kodak Film Chevrolet	409	$17,900	Handling
24	33	22	Bobby Labonte	Maxwell House Coffee Ford	397	$7,925	Accident
25	24	44	Rick Wilson	STP Pontiac	392	$9,630	Running
26	9	5	Ricky Rudd	Tide Chevrolet	369	$12,500	Accident
27	23	27	Hut Stricklin	McDonald's Ford	352	$12,425	Running
28	26	33	Harry Gant	Skoal Bandit Chevrolet	329	$16,775	Running
29	16	83	Lake Speed	Purex Detergent Ford	305	$7,745	Engine
30	20	11	Bill Elliott	Budweiser Ford	303	$17,620	Accident
31	29	41	Phil Parsons	Manhein Auctions Chevrolet	254	$8,395	Engine
32	22	18	Dale Jarrett	Interstate Batteries Chevrolet	207	$15,420	Parked
33	13	90	Bobby Hillin	Hellig-Meyers Ford	119	$6,420	Accident
34	7	25	Ken Schrader	Kodiak Chevrolet	51	$10,970	Accident
35	11	68	Bobby Hamilton	Country Time Ford	27	$7,025	Engine

AVERAGE SPEED: 84.730 mph
TIME OF RACE: 3 hours, 8 minutes, 23 seconds
MARGIN OF VICTORY: 0.82 seconds
LEAD CHANGES: 19 among 10 drivers

CAUTION FLAGS: 17 for 87 laps
CROWD ESTIMATE: 68,000 (RECORD)

UNOFFICIAL RESULTS OF THE $897,387, FOOD CITY 500, NASCAR WINSTON CUP RACE
BRISTOL INTERNATIONAL RACEWAY, BRISTOL, TN, APRIL 10, 1994

Finishing Position	Starting Position	Car Number	Driver	Team	Laps	Money	Running/Reason Out
1	24	3	Dale Earnhardt	Goodwrench Chevrolet	500	$72,570	Running
2	22	25	Ken Schrader	Kodiak Chevrolet	500	$40,445	Running
3	13	15	Lake Speed	Quality Care Ford	500	$35,020	Running
4	27	7	Geoff Bodine	Exide Batteries Ford	499	$24,356	Running
5	23	30	Michael Waltrip	Pennzoil Pontiac	497	$20,135	Running
6	9	22	Bobby Labonte	Maxwell Coffee House Pontiac	496	$18,785	Running
7	2	2	Rusty Wallace	Miller Genuine Draft Ford	494	$23,385	Running
8	18	4	Sterling Marlin	Kodak Chevrolet	491	$20,285	Running
9	34	40	Bobby Hamilton	Kendall Oil Pontiac	488	$17,280	Running
10	29	71	Dave Marcis	STG/Tri City Aviation Pontiac	486	$15,280	Running
11	31	77	Greg Sacks	USAir/Jasper Ford	482	$9,480	Running
12	30	29	Steve Grissom	Diamond Ridge Chevrolet	480	$10,230	Running
13	19	26	Brett Bodine	Quaker State Ford	478	$16,155	Running
14	26	23	Hut Stricklin	Smokin' Joe's Racing Ford	478	$8,905	Running
15	31	17	Darrell Waltrip	Western Auto Chevrolet	476	$15,755	Running
16	6	41	Joe Nemecheck	Meineke Mufflers Chevrolet	473	$11,480	Running
17	33	43	Wally Dallenbach	STP Pontiac	464	$11,330	Running
18	10	21	Morgan Shepherd	Citgo Ford	457	$18,580	Running
19	5	16	Ted Musgrave	Family Channel Ford	431	$15,170	Running
20	14	42	Kyle Petty	Mello Yello Pontiac	426	$19,511	Running
21	3	6	Mark Martin	Valvoline Ford	425	$20,405	Accident

22	4	24	Jeff Gordon	DuPont Chevrolet	425	$14,855	Accident
23	1	12	Chuck Brown	Masterbuilt/WBF Ford	393	$19,105	Running
24	12	5	Terry Labonte	Kellogg's Corn Flakes Chevrolet	373	$18,130	Running
25	21	31	Ward Burton	Hardee's Chevrolet	368	$8,585	Running
26	8	75	Todd Bodine	Factory Stores Ford	358	$10,355	Running
27	17	98	Derrike Cope	Fingerhut Ford	276	$10,231	Running
28	25	90	Mike Wallace	Hellig-Meyers Ford	262	$10,080	Engine
29	28	1	Rick Mast	Skoal Classic Ford	222	$9,950	Accident
30	15	11	Bill Elliott	Budweiser Ford	198	$13,625	Accident
31	35	8	Jeff Burton	Raybestos Ford	197	$12,625	Accident
32	11	10	Ricky Rudd	Tide Ford	187	$6,625	Accident
33	7	28	Ernie Irvan	Texaco Havoline Ford	167	$18,225	Engine
34	32	32	Dick Trickle	Active Trucking Chevrolet	164	$6,625	Engine
35	16	27	Jimmy Spencer	McDonald's Ford	159	$6,625	Cylinder Head
36	36	18	Dale Jarrett	Interstate Batteries Chevrolet	66	$12,025	Accident
37	20	33	Harry Gant	Skoal Bandit Chevrolet	10	$10,625	Accident

Average speed: 89.647 mph
Time of race: 2 hours, 58 minutes, 22 seconds
Lead Changes: 11 among 6 drivers
Caution flags: 10 for 75 laps
Estimated crowd: 73000 (RECORD)

UNOFFICIAL RESULTS FOR THE FOOD CITY 500 NASCAR WINSTON CUP RACE (500 Laps)
BRISTOL INTERNATIONAL RACEWAY, BRISTOL, TN, 1995

Finishing Position	Starting Position	Car Number	Driver	Team	Laps	Money	Running or Reason Out
1	2	24	Jeff Gordon	DuPont Chevrolet	500	$67,645	Running
2	9	2	Rusty Wallace	Miller Genuine Draft Ford	500	$42,045	Running
3	12	17	Darrell Waltrip	Western Auto Chevrolet	500	$35,845	Running
4	17	43	Bobby Hamilton	STP Pontiac	500	$28,631	Running
5	13	10	Ricky Rudd	Tide Ford	500	$32,260	Running
6	19	28	Dale Jarrett	Texaco/Havoline Ford	500	$27,660	Running
7	21	5	Terry Labonte	Kellogg's Corn Flakes Chevrolet	499	$28,060	Running
8	1	6	Mark Martin	Valvoline Ford	499	$44,860	Running
9	31	4	Sterling Marlin	Kodak Chevrolet	499	$27,055	Running
10	18	33	Robert Pressley	Skoal Bandit Chevrolet	498	$24,605	Running
11	34	29	Steve Grissom	Meineke Chevrolet	498	$15,955	Running
12	24	33	Randy Lajoie	MBNA America Pontiac	497	$21,105	Running
13	4	12	Derrike Cope	Straight Arrow Products Ford	496	$15,430	Running
14	20	94	Bill Elliott	McDonald's Ford	496	$10,980	Running
15	30	1	Rick Mast	Skoal Racing Ford	496	$20,530	Running
16	23	23	Jimmy Spencer	Camel Ford	495	$14,755	Running
17	28	9	Lake Speed	Spam/Melling Ford	495	$10,705	Running
18	6	16	Ted Musgrave	Family Channel Ford	495	$19,455	Running
19	8	37	John Andretti	Kmart/Little Caesar's Ford	492	$10,645	Running
20	32	21	Morgan Shepherd	Citgo Ford	492	$20,536	Running
21	35	31	Ward Burton	Hardee's Chevrolet	489	$10,380	Running

22	33	30	Michael Waltrip	Pennzoil Pontiac	489	$18,930	Running
23	11	7	Geoff Bodine	Exide Batteries Ford	488	$24,980	Running
24	26	77	Davy Jones	Jasper Engines/USAir Ford	486	$13,705	Running
25	25	3	Dale Earnhardt	GM Goodwrench Chevrolet	479	$36,360	Running
26	27	25	Ken Schrader	Budweiser Chevrolet	475	$18,530	Running
27	14	11	Brett Bodine	Lowe's Ford	460	$23,106	Running
28	10	8	Jeff Burton	Raybestos Ford	413	$18,355	Running
29	7	41	Ricky Craven	Kodiak Chevrolet	407	$13,225	Running
30	22	15	Dick Trickle	Quality Care Ford	407	$17,800	Running
31	16	32	Chuck Bown	Active Trucking Chevrolet	395	$12,200	Running
32	5	18	Bobby Labonte	Interstate Batteries Chevrolet	392	$16,700	Running
33	29	75	Todd Bodine	Factory Stores Ford	392	$16,200	Running
34	36	71	Dave Marcis	Terramite Chevrolet	354	$9,200	Running
35	3	42	Kyle Petty	Coors Light Pontiac	276	$14,000	Accident
36	15	40	Greg Sacks	Kendall Oil Pontiac	212	$13,700	Engine

Average Speed: 92.011 mph
Estimated Attendance: 76,000
Time of Race: 2 hours, 53 minutes, 47 seconds
Margin of Victory: 5.74 seconds
Lead changes: 12 among 5 drivers
Caution flags: 7 for 65 laps

UNOFFICIAL RESULTS FOR THE GOODY'S 500, NASCAR WINSTON CUP RACE 266.5 Miles (500 Laps) on the .533 Mile, BRISTOL INTERNATIONAL RACEWAY, BRISTOL, TN, AUGUST 27, 1994

Finishing Position	Starting Position	Car Number	Driver	Team/Car	Laps	Money	Running or Reason Out
1	4	2	Rusty Wallace	Miller Genuine Draft Ford	500	$53,015	Running
2	8	6	Mark Martin	Valvoline Oil Ford	500	$35,915	Running
3	14	3	Dale Earnhardt	GM Goodwrench Chevrolet	500	$33,265	Running
4	16	17	Darrell Waltrip	Western Auto Chevrolet	500	$28,730	Running
5	11	11	Bill Elliott	Budweiser Ford	500	$22,275	Running
6	24	4	Sterling Marlin	Kodak Film Chevrolet	500	$21,265	Running
7	28	30	Michael Waltrip	Pennzoil Pontiac	500	$17,965	Running
8	36	75	Todd Bodine	Factory Stores Ford	500	$15,465	Running
9	1	33	Harry Gant	Skoal Bandit Chevrolet	499	$23,540	Running
10	9	1	Rick Mast	Red Food Skoal Ford	499	$19,040	Running
11	18	16	Ted Musgrave	The Family Channel Ford	499	$16,340	Running
12	33	10	Ricky Rudd	Tide Ford	499	$16,540	Running
13	15	28	Kenny Wallace	Texaco Ford	499	$20,490	Running
14	22	26	Brett Bodine	Quaker State Ford	497	$15,540	Running
15	32	42	Kyle Petty	Mello Yello Pontiac	497	$19,935	Running
16	19	12	Derrike Cope	Straight Arrow Ford	496	$15,085	Running
17	6	32	Dick Trickle	Active Trucking Chevrolet	496	$10,935	Running
18	31	25	Morgan Shepherd	Citgo Ford	495	$18,285	Running

20	20	8	Jeff Burton	Raybestos Ford	490	$16,285	Running
21	25	98	Jeremy Mayfield	Fingerhut Ford	486	$10,935	Running
22	34	52	Brad Teague	NAPA Ford	478	$8,085	Running
23	2	7	Geoff Bodine	Exide Batteries Ford	478	$17,235	Piston
24	27	90	Mike Wallace	Hellig-Meyers Ford	456	$10,060	Accident
25	35	15	Lake Speed	Ford Quality Care Ford	409	$17,915	Accident
26	29	18	Dale Jarrett	Interstate Batteries Chevrolet	388	$19,285	Accident
27	13	77	Greg Sacks	USAir Jasper Engines Ford	373	$9,862	Rear End
28	17	40	Bobby Hamilton	Kendall Oil Pontiac	298	$13,810	Accident
29	5	41	Joe Nemechek	Meineke Muffler Chevrolet	286	$9,285	Accident
30	23	43	John Andretti	STP Pontiac	261	$7,735	Accident
31	10	22	Bobby Labonte	Maxwell Coffee House Pontiac	258	$11,735	Accident
32	12	24	Jeff Gordon	DuPont Chevrolet	222	$17,735	Accident
33	3	5	Terry Labonte	Kellogg's Chevrolet	115	$18,035	Accident
34	30	29	Steve Grissom	Diamond Ridge Chevrolet	108	$7,735	Overheating
35	26	23	Hut Stricklin	Camel Cigarettes Ford	86	$7,735	Accident
36	7	31	Ward Burton	Hardee's Chevrolet	49	$7,735	Engine

Average Speed: 91.363
Estimated Attendance: 74,800
Time of Race: 2 hours, 55 minutes, 1 second
Margin of Victory: 0.16 seconds
Lead Changes: 16 among 10 drivers
Caution Flags: 12 for 73 laps

UNOFFICIAL RESULTS FOR THE GOODY'S 500, NASCAR WINSTON CUP RACE
BRISTOL INTERNATIONAL RACEWAY, BRISTOL, TN, AUGUST 1995

Finishing Position	Starting Position	Car Number	Driver	Team	Laps	Money	Running or Reason Out
1	2	5	Terry Labonte	Kellogg's Chevrolet	500	$66,940	Running
2	7	3	Dale Earnhardt	GM Goodwrench Service Chevrolet	500	$66,890	Running
3	16	28	Dale Jarrett	Texaco Havoline Ford	500	$39,390	Running
4	20	17	Darrell Waltrip	Western Auto Chevrolet	500	$32,780	Running
5	1	6	Mark Martin	Valvoline Ford	500	$41,775	Running
6	4	24	Jeff Gordon	DuPont Chevrolet	500	$27,865	Running
7	19	4	Sterling Marlin	Kodak Film Chevrolet	500	$26,140	Running
8	27	90	Mike Wallace	Hellig-Meyers Ford	500	$14,840	Running
9	18	8	Jeff Burton	Raybestos Ford	500	$22,515	Running
10	10	12	Derrike Cope	Straight Arrow Ford	499	$20,565	Running
11	28	18	Bobby Labonte	Interstate Batteries Chevrolet	499	$25,015	Running
12	13	7	Geoff Bodine	Exide Batteries Ford	499	$26,415	Running
13	9	16	Ted Musgrave	The Family Channel Ford	497	$21,065	Running
14	25	25	Ken Schrader	Budweiser Ford	497	$20,815	Running
15	3	30	Michael Waltrip	Pennzoil Pontiac	497	$21,960	Running
16	12	87	Joe Nemecheck	Burger King Chevrolet	496	$15,260	Running
17	29	21	Morgan Shepherd	Citgo Ford	495	$20,110	Running
18	26	23	Jimmy	Camel	494	$14,860	Running

				Spencer	Cigarettes Ford			
19	34	37	John Andretti	Kmart Little Caesars Ford	476	$14,750	Running	
20	31	43	Bobby Hamilton	STP Pontiac	466	$16,360	Running	
21	5	2	Rusty Wallace	Miller Genuine Draft Ford	454	$26,110	Running	
22	23	29	Steve Grissom	Meineke Chevrolet	454	$14,360	Running	
23	22	94	Bill Elliott	McDonald's Ford	453	$14,210	Running	
24	14	33	Robert Pressley	Ingles Skoal Chevrolet	438	$20,035	Running	
25	21	31	Greg Sacks	Hardee's Chevrolet	422	$14,590	Running	
26	24	1	Rick Mast	Skoal Racing Ford	412	$18,760	Running	
27	32	71	Dave Marcis	Olive Garden Chevrolet	404	$13,637	Accident	
28	33	11	Brett Bodine	Lowe's Ford	404	$23,585	Running	
29	36	9	Lake Speed	Spam Melling Ford	391	$14,560	Accident	
30	30	98	Jeremy Mayfield	RCA Ford	382	$13,010	Accident	
31	15	40	Rick Bickle	Kendall Oil Pontiac	368	$15,510	Engine	
32	6	41	Ricky Craven	Kodiak Chevrolet	306	$11,010	Accident	
33	11	26	Hut Stricklin	Quaker State Ford	253	$15,510	Accident	
34	17	22	Ward Burton	MBNA Pontiac	250	$15,510	Engine	
35	35	15	Dick Trickle	Quality Care Ford	233	$15,510	Accident	
36	8	10	Ricky Rudd	Tide Ford	138	$23,510	Accident	

Average Speed: 81.979 MPH
Estimated Crowd Attendance: 79,000
Time of Race: 3 hours, 15 minutes, 3 seconds
Margin of Victory: 0.10 seconds
Lead Changes: 16 among 10 drivers
Caution Flags: 15 for 106 laps

NASCAR WINSTON CUP RACE NUMBER 6 - 1989 SEASON
VALLEYDALE MEATS 500 – BRISTOL INTERNATIONAL RACEWAY, BRISTOL, TN
.533 Mile Paved Speedway, April 9, 1989 - 266.5 M- 500 L- Purse: $441,167

Finish Position	Starting Position	Car Number	Driver	Team	Laps	Winston Cup Points	Bonus Points	Total Money Won	Reason Out of Race
1	8	27	Rusty Wallace	Kodiak Pontiac	500	180	5	$48,750	"
2	11	17	Darrell Waltrip	Tide Chevrolet	500	170		$28,900	"
3	2	5	Geoff Bodine	Levi Garrett Chevrolet	500	170	5	$21,950	"
4	31	28	Davey Allison	Havoline Ford	500	165	5	$17,802	"
5	27	84	Dick Trickle	Miller High Life Buick	500	155		$12,950	"
6	1	6	Mark Martin	Stroh's Light Ford	500	155	5	$13,975	"
7	21	88	Greg Sacks	Crisco Pontiac	500	156	10	$9,300	"
8	18	26	Ricky Rudd	Quaker State Buick	500	142		$7,325	"
9	16	9	Bill Elliott	Coors Ford	500	143	5	$13,150	"
10	11	33	Harry Gant	Skoal Bandit Oldsmobile	500	139	5	$10,350	"
11	7	30	Michael Waltrip	Country Time Lemonade Pontiac	499	130		$6,500	"
12	29	21	Neil Bonnett	Citgo Ford	499	132	5	$6,075	"
13	23	31	Jim Sauter	Slender You Figure Salons Pontiac	498	124		$6,300	"
14	15	66	Rick Mast	Mach One Racing Chevrolet	496	126	5	$5,800	"
15	14	94	Sterling Marlin	Sunoco Oldsmobile	493	123	5	$6,930	"
16	5	3	Dale Earnhart	GM Goodwrench Chevrolet	492	120	5	$21,280	"
17	28	67	Brad Teague	You Can Rent Pontiac	488	112		$2,480	Oil Line
18	32	16	Larry Pearson	Chattanooga Chew Buick	480	109		$2,430	Running

19	12	23	Eddie Bierschwale	Americraft Oldsmobile	479	106		$2,390	"
20	3	7	Alan Kulwicki	Zerex Ford	458	108	5	$6,075	"
21	4	4	Rick Wilson	Kodak Film Oldsmobile	442	105	5	$4,710	"
22	20	29	Dale Jarrett	Hardee's Pontiac	440	97		$4,520	"
23	6	55	Phil Parsons	Crown Oldsmobile	420	94		$4,395	Accident
24	19	11	Terry Labonte	Budweiser Ford	400	91		$7,825	Running
25	30	83	Lake Speed	Bull's Eye Barbecue Sauce Oldsmobile	397	88		$4,405	"
26	10	75	Morgan Shepherd	Valvoline Pontiac	234	90	5	$8,745	Accident
27	22	8	Bobby Hillin	Miller High Life Buick	215	87	5	$4,160	Accident
28	26	57	Hut Stricklin	Heinz Ketchup Pontiac	167	89		$1,970	Accident
29	25	2	Ernie Irvan	Kroger Pontiac	167	81	5	$2,535	Accident
30	24	15	Brett Bodine	Motorcraft Ford	167	73		$3,450	Accident
31	9	51	Butch Miller	Phoenix Construct Inn Chevrolet	80	70		$1,950	Accident
32	17	25	Ken Schrader	Folger's Coffee Chevrolet	35	67		$7,650	Accident

Time of Race: 3 hours, 30 minutes, 18 seconds   Average Speed: 76.034 MPH
Margin of Victory: .26 seconds
Busch Pole Award: Mark Martin (Stroh's Light Ford, 120.278 mph (15.953)- TRACK RECORD
True Value Hard Charger Award: Geoff Bodine (Levi Garrett Chevrolet)- Sacks, Earnhardt, Gant, Martin
Van Camp's Determination Award: Mark Martin (Stroh's Light Ford)- Greg Sacks
TRW Mechanic of Race- Bob Clark, Slender You Figure Salons Pontiac
Heinz Ketchup Award Winner: Davey Allison, Halvoline Ford
Goody's Headache Award: Sterling Marlin (Sunoco Oldsmobile)
Right Guard Halfway Challenge Award: Dale Earhardt (GM Goodwrench Chevrolet)
Caution Flags: 20 for 98 laps (37-43, 59-65, 83-84, 95-97, 126-128, 151-157, 162-165, 169-181, 217-227, 239-245, 257-258, 265-268, 285-287, 313-315, 365-368, 377-378, 424-430, 457-458, 476-477, 481-485

NASCAR WINSTON CUP RACE NUMBER 6 - 1990 SEASON
VALLEYDALE MEATS 500 - Bristol International Speedway
Bristol, Tennessee - .533 Mile Paved Speedway, April 8, 1990 - 266.50 M- 500 L- Purse: $465,992

Finishing Position	Starting Position	Car Number	Driver	Team	Laps	Winston Cup Points	Bonus Points	Total Money Won	Reason Out of Race
1	19	28	Davey Allison	Havoline Ford	500	180	5	$50,300	"
2	3	5	Mark Martin	Folger's Coffee Ford	500	170		$31,300	
3	13	1	Ricky Rudd	Levi Garrett Chevrolet	500	165		$19,775	
4	14	75	Terry Labonte	Skoal Oldsmobile	500	160		$13,500	
5	25	94	Rick Wilson	Dinner Bell Foods Oldsmobile	500	155		$13,857	
6	17	25	Ken Schrader	Kodiak Chevrolet	500	150		$11,675	
7	5	94	Sterling Marlin	Sunoco Oldsmobile	500	151	5	$8,850	
8	7	15	Morgan Shepherd	Motorcraft Ford	499	142		$8,475	
9	10	17	Darrell Waltrip	Tide Chevrolet	499	148	10	$25,500	
10	4	42	Kyle Petty	PEAK Pontiac	499	139	5	$11,900	
11	12	21	Dale Jarrett	Citgo Ford	493	135	5	$8,300	
12	8	2	Rick Mast	US Racing Pontiac	489	127		$8,225	
13	6	66	Dick Trickle	Phillips TropArtic Pontiac	488	124		$7,950	
14	32	98	Butch Hiller	Food City Chevrolet	486	121		$4,000	
15	16	71	Dave Marcis	Big Apple Market Chevrolet	471	123	5	$7,025	
16	1	4	Ernie Irvan	Kodak Film Oldsmobile	471	120	5	$8,800	
17	11	9	Bill Elliott	Coors Ford	465	112		$10,990	
18	26	57	Jimmy Spencer	Heinz Pontiac	456	109		$6,725	
19	9	3	Dale Earnhardt	GM Goodwrench	451	106		$5,725	

20	20	30	Michael Waltrip	Chevrolet Maxwell House Coffee Pontiac	442	103	5	$	
21	15	8	Bobby Hillin	SNICKERS Buick	433	105			
22	18	26	Brett Bodine	Quaker State Buick	421	97			
23	29	12	Mike Alexander	Reybeston Brakes Buick	394	94			
24	2	11	Geoff Bodine	Budweiser Ford	383	96	5		
25	31	33	Phil Parsons	Skoal Oldsmobile	342	88			
26	28	43	Richard Petty	STP Pontiac	328	85			
27	30	70	J.D. McDuffle	Rumple Furniture Pontiac	290	82			
28	23	27	Rusty Wallace	Miller Genuine Draft Pontiac	220	79			
29	27	52	Jimmy Means	Alka-Seltzer Pontiac	202	76			
30	24	20	Rob Moroso	Crown Oldsmobile	169	73			
31	21	7	Alan Kulwicki	Zerex Ford	126	70			
32	22	10	Derrike Cope	Purolator Chevrolet	54	67			

NASCAR WINSTON CUP RACE #6—1991 Season
VALLEYDALE MEATS 500, BRISTOL INTERNATIONAL RACEWAY
BRISTOL, TN, .533 Mile Paved Speedway, April 14, 1991 - 266.5 M -500L - Purse: $529,181

Final Position	Starting Position	Car Number	Driver	Team	Laps	Winston Cup Points	Bonus Points	Total Money Won	Reason Out of the Race
1	1	2	Rusty Wallace	Miller Genuine Draft Pontiac	500	180	5	$51,300	Running
2	8	4	Ernie Irvan	Kodak Film Chevrolet	500	175	5	$31,925	
3	3	28	Davey Allison	Havoline Ford	500	170	5	$26,000	
4	6	6	Mark Martin	Folger's Coffee Ford	500	165	5	$18,950	
5	4	5	Ricky Rudd	Tide Chevrolet	500	165	10	$37,950	
6	22	17	Darrell Waltrip	Western Auto Chevrolet	500	150		$7,525	
7	18	21	Dale Jarrett	Citgo Ford	500	146		$10,775	
8	20	98	Jimmy Spencer	Food City Chevrolet	500	142		$10,175	
9	30	94	Terry Labonte	Sunoco Oldsmobile	500	138		$9,575	
10	26	15	Morgan Shepherd	Motorcraft Ford	498	134		$14,275	
11	10	33	Harry Gant	Skoal Bandit Oldsmobile	498	135	5	$9,375	
12	27	55	Ted Musgrave	Alka-Seltzer Pontiac	498	127		$8,275	
13	23	75	Joe Ruttman	Dinner Bell Foods Oldsmobile	498	124		$8,150	
14	31	19	Chad Little	Tyson Food Ford	497	126	5	$6,400	
15	19	20	Bobby Hillin	Moroso Racing Oldsmobile	497	118		$6,800	
16	13	12	Hut Stricklin	Raybestos Buick	496	115		$7,475	
17	33	43	Richard Petty	STP Pontiac	496	112		$7,225	
18	9	1	Rick Mast	Skoal	492	109		$7,025	

				Oldsmobile					
19	17	24	Mickey Gibbs	Team III Pontiac	492	106		$4,665	
20	2	3	Dale Earnhardt	GM Goodwrench Chevrolet	484	103		$15,525	
21	12	42	Kyle Petty	Mello Yello Pontiac	480	100		$10,125	
22	7	26	Brett Bodine	Quaker State Buick	471	97		$6,675	
23	25	30	Michael Waltrip	Pennzoil Pontiac	463	94		$6,650	
24	11	11	Geoff Bodine	Budweiser Ford	461	91		$11,750	
25	24	66	Lake Speed	TropArtic Pontiac	455	88		$6,480	
26	5	7	Alan Kulwicki	Hooter's Ford	434	85		$9,875	
27	15	22	Sterling Marlin	Maxwell House Coffee Ford	421	82		$5,150	Accident
28	29	9	Bill Elliott	Coors Light Ford	406	79		$9,800	Running
29	14	25	Ken Schrader	Kodiak Chevrolet	314	81	5	$6,220	Accident
30	21	34	Dick Trickle	Allen's Glass Buick	314	73		$4,025	Ignition
31	28	68	Bobby Hamilton	Country Time Oldsmobile	124	70		$4,275	Engine Failure
32	32	10	Derrick Cope	Purolator Chevrolet	80	67		$11,125	Accident
33	16	8	Rick Wilson	SNICKERS Buick	78	64		$5,850	Overheating

Time of Race: 3 hours, 39 minutes, 37 seconds   Average Speed: 72.809 mph
Margin of Victory: 1 foot
Busch Pole Award: Rusty Wallace, Miller Genuine Draft Pontiac, 118.051 mph (16.254 seconds)
Right Guard Halfway Challenge: Ricky Rudd, Tide Chevrolet
True Value Hard Charger Award: Ricky Rudd, Tide Chevrolet (Allison, Irvan, Wallace, Gant)
Gatorade Circle of Champions Award: Rusty Wallace, Miller Genuine Draft Pontiac
Tyson Lickety Split Award: Ricky Rudd, Tide Chevrolet, 112.474 mph—lap 203
Michigan/MC Cord Engine Builder of the Race Award: David Evans, Miller Genuine Draft Pontiac-NOT ELIGIBLE)
Plasti-Kote Winning Finish Award: Jimmy Makar, Miller Genuine Draft Pontiac- NOT ELIGIBLE
Dinner Bell Top Dog Award: Rusty Wallace, Miller Genuine Draft Pontiac—NOT ELIGIBLE

Western Auto Mechanic of the Race: Larry McReynolds, Havoline Ford
Budget Team Service Award: Penske Racing—NOT ELIGIBLE
Goody's Headache Award: Sterling Marlin, Maxwell Coffee House Ford
UNOCAL Challenge Winner: Rusty Wallace, Miller Genuine Draft Pontiac, $22,800
CAUTION FLAGS: 19 for 133 laps (18-21, 32-35, 39-45, 50-52, 55-61, 76-78, 82-90, 104-106, 160-167, 187-194, 196-200, 256-263, 288-295, 301-305, 369-375, 406-413, 423-438, 449-462, 472-477)

CHAPTER 12

My take on NASCAR Drivers

Fans and friends would frequently ask me about this or that driver. Is so-and-so a good guy? Is so-and-so in real life like he appears on TV?

So, dear readers, the best thing I can do for you is go down the driver's list and briefly tell you my personal experiences with each driver that ran Bristol International Raceway during my tenure. I'll rate my experiences with them – from my public relations standpoint – on a scale from 1-10, with 10 being the highest.

Mark Martin, Batesville, Ark.: Mark was a driver's driver. For what he lacked in stature at 5-foot-6, he made up for in the gym. His biceps were as big as my thighs. He worked out religiously and was the guy who would stay for as long as you wanted him to at press conferences and personal appearances. He retired in 2013 after an illustrious career in both Winston/Sprint Cup and Grand National competition. Rating:10

Alan Kulwicki, Greenfield, Wisc.: Alan was an intelligent college engineering graduate who liked to work on his car rather than participate in the press "stuff." He was subdued and answered questions in short monotone sentences. When he won the 1991 Bud 500 night race, he criticized us for the track conditions saying the concrete surface was too rough. Really? I wanted to take the check away from him in Victory Lane. Rating: 5

Dale Earnhardt, Kannapolis, N.C.: A happy-go-lucky fun-loving guy. Before every race he'd come to my office, as he put it: "To check on my trophy." You'd never know he was NASCAR's biggest star at the time. I could always count on a warm welcome in his motor home. And, he was always animated and a great interview with the press. Rating: 10

Michael Waltrip, Owensboro, Ky: If NASCAR ever promotes a Batman movie, using drivers, Michael should be cast as The Joker. He told me a story one time when, according to him, he and Kyle Petty picked up Alan Kulwicki and hung him on the back of the door in the infield media center at Talladega. Waltrip stands over 6 feet tall as does Petty. Kulwicki was 5-foot-8. I snickered at the story. Alan said later it wasn't true. I still believe the pranksters! Rating: 9

Geoff Bodine, Chemung, N.Y: Ever accommodating as the driver of the Budweiser Ford, Geoff's problem with the Southern Circuit was he spelled his name wrong, it's Jeff, not Geoff and he was from Chemung, New York. His autograph wasn't hotly sought after at Food City Race Night. Smart guy. Designed a competitive sled for Olympic competition. Offered me a job as his PR guy once. Never thought he was serious and I wasn't interested anyway. Rating: 6

Rick Wilson, Bartow, Fla: Known by some fans as "Wreck Wilson," Rick was a nice enough guy. He just had a hard time not wrecking or causing wrecks at Bristol. However, he did have some success on the high banks and won some races. Rating: 6

Rusty Wallace, St. Louis, Mo. Rusty was the winner of the first Winston Cup event I was involved in. He was funny and could get around BMS better than anyone except Darrell Waltrip. I became a Rusty Wallace fan because of the first impression he made on me during my very first event. Later, he would be the annual guest at the speedway's Christmas party at the Bristol Country Club. Whenever I asked him for his participation in events, press luncheons, or fan autographs for fans he was always accommodating. Rating: 10

Morgan Shepherd, Conover, N.C.: Nice enough guy. He agreed to an appearance at a relatively new local college, Northeast State Community College. For the day he "taught" the automotive class and knew all there was to know about engines and hung around with the students, signing autograph long after the bell rang ending class. Rating: 7

Harry Gant, Taylorsville, N.C.: After winning a race at Bristol, during the trophy presentation in Victory Lane, I asked Harry how he would be celebrating. "Celebrating?" he asked. "I've got to put a roof on a house tomorrow!" When he wasn't racing, Harry was working in construction. He was one of the most admired racers in his era – always a bright smile and a positive attitude. I liked Harry Gant a lot both as a racer and person. Rating: 9

Darrell Waltrip, Franklin, Tenn.: Whenever I think of Darrell Waltrip I think of his win at Daytona where he shouted live on a CBS broadcast, "I just won the Daytona 500. I just won the Daytona 500!" And then he did that cheesy dance and slammed down his helmet. The "winningest" driver in Bristol Motor Speedway history was always thoughtful and kind, and he was the real deal. You'd think that 11 wins at the World's Fastest Half-Mile would make him cocky but that was the furthest thing from the truth. While looking for a seat at one of the annual awards banquet, he motioned for me to sit at his table and we had a nice, hour-long conversation. Rating: 10

Ken Schrader, Fenton, Mo.: Ken would be racing somewhere before our events and it didn't matter if it was an open-wheel car or a go-cart. He was grounded and seemed to be surprised to be as popular as he was. Like many drivers, however, I really never got to know Ken personally. Rating: 7

Sterling Marlin, Columbia, Tenn.: Sterling has a signature Southern drawl and I use to like to hear him talk. He crashed at Bristol once, his car became engulfed in flames and he suffered severe burns. Carrier and I visited with him in the local hospital where he was placed in ICU. Even after the crash, he had nothing but good things to say about Bristol and he enjoyed success on the track. Rating: 8

Bill Elliott, Dawsonville, Ga.: I was very surprised to find Elliott to be somewhat of a jerk. The "Most Popular Driver" – voted by fans on several occasions – really thought he was something. Because of this, during his assigned day at our track to help promote our race, instead of letting him go relax after our press luncheon, which was customary, I had him make appearances at several other places. We hit every AM radio station in the region. After purposely getting lost on the way to Kingsport, I dropped him off at his hotel at 8 p.m. Rating: 2 (because nobody deserves a 1)

Ricky Rudd, Chesapeake, Va.: He was driving the Quaker State car when I met him to open the gate for a tire-testing session. He was always approachable, and on that day, he invited me to have lunch in the media center after the morning tire test was over. He always had time for the press during his visit to Bristol. Rating: 9

Terry Labonte, Corpus Christi, Texas: When Dale Earnhardt wrecked him on the last lap of the 1995 Goody's 500 Night Race, I was waiting for a fight to erupt in the infield. Instead, Terry just said, "That's racin'!" with a big grin on his face. Enough said. Rating: 9

Dale Jarrett, Conover, N.C.: Dale is a gentleman's gentleman and I think he got that from his NASCAR champion dad, Ned. Once in Victory

Lane, after winning a Busch Grand National Race, I remember Dale stayed on stage until the last photographer got his picture and the last question was asked by the last reporter. It didn't matter to him if you were representing the *Elizabethton (Tenn.) Star* or *USA Today*. It was obvious he loved what he was doing. It's a pleasure to watch him today and a television commentator. Rating: 10

Brett Bodine, Chemung, N.Y.: Even though he never won at Bristol, he generally qualified well and always ran hard. Brett went on to work for NASCAR after sponsorship money dried up. The middle brother to Geoff and Todd, Brett was fun to be around. Rating: 8

Ernie Irvan, Modesto, Calif.: When Ernie landed the Morgan-McClure ride, based in Abingdon, Va., BMS became his "home track." When he won the 1990 Busch 500, he criticized the track's surface in post-race interviews with the press, which didn't sit well with me. But, when it came to making appearances on behalf of the track, he was always very accommodating. Rating: 7

Dick Trickle, Wisconsin Rapids, Wisc.: What can you say about a guy who frequently lit up a cigarette while racing? Dick was a fun-loving guy who joked around all the time. I was sorry to hear of his passing in 2013. Rating: 10

Brad Teague, Johnson City, Tenn.: If Brad had secured sponsorship for his car, he would have gone a long way in NASCAR. A local celebrity, he recently quit the sport after competing since 1982. Rating: 9

Davey Allison, Hueytown, Ala.: Davey frequently came by my office during race weekends to ask if there was anything he could do for me and the track. He was a class act and if he had not been killed in a tragic helicopter accident, he would have won a bunch more races. Rating: 10

CHAPTER 13

Richard Petty calls it quits

As track spokesman and general manager for BIR, whenever there was a NASCAR meeting, death in the racing community, special event or other announcement that might affect the track, I was the one to attend those meetings or funerals.

On Sept. 19, 1991 Carrier received a Western Union Mailgram from Ruder-Finn Inc., a New York City public relations firm representing Richard Petty Enterprises. It read:

> Dear Mr. Carrier:
> On Tuesday, October 1, 1991 Richard Petty and STP will make a news announcement of great importance to his fans and the racing fraternity.
> The announcement will take place at 10:30 a.m. at the Richard Petty Museum on the grounds of Petty Enterprises in Level Cross, N.C.
> An informal lunch will be served after the press conference. If you're planning to attend, or have questions concerning lodging or direction to the Petty Museum, please RSVP to:
> Tom Crane/Richard Wagner

Ruder-Finn, Inc.
212-593-6400

So, in the wee hours of Oct. 1, I set out from Johnson City to Level Cross, N.C., in the track pace car with an atlas in hand. I still have the yellowed Western Union Mailgram and was surprised to find that I had typed my experience that day at the Richard Petty Museum and had attached it to the document.

Here's what I had written:

On Tuesday, October 1, 1991, Richard Petty announced his retirement at his museum in Level Cross, North Carolina. It was a bright, sunny day and "The King" of stock car racing welcomed a legion of reporters, track representatives, elected officials and special guests from all over the country. I sat in the third row during this emotional day. The press had speculated for weeks what the announcement would be. Some had Petty running for United States Senate, while others had him in a future ride for Chrysler.

Joining Petty on the podium was Gov. Jim Martin of North Carolina; NASCAR President Bill France Jr.; Petty's sponsors' representatives; his son, Kyle; his three sisters; and his wife, Linda. It was indeed his announcement to quit driving a stock car but he wasn't getting out of racing.

He announced that 1992 would be his last year behind the wheel and he would be calling it his "Fan Appreciation Tour," whereby fans would be given ample chances to see him both behind the wheel and in person at many special events. After 1992, he said he'd be a car owner and stay in the sport as long as he was able ... and hopefully for as long as he would live.

I was one of about 200 people in attendance to witness one of the biggest announcements in racing history.

"This whole situation came up about a year ago," Petty told the crowd. "It's not a farewell tour because I'm not going anywhere."

Petty drove for 34 seasons and is a member of the NASCAR Hall of Fame. His last win came in 1984, when he won at Daytona in front of thousands of fans, including then-President Ronald Reagan, who was campaigning for a second term. He congratulated Petty on the win and then took off in Air Force One, which later became a popular photo that was gobbled up by race fans all over the world.

During my tenure at Bristol International Raceway, Petty's best finish was 12th however, in his career he had 37 Top 10s at BIR. I remember him as a great competitor, fan favorite and accommodating with his time and requests for autographs. With his signature cowboy hat and dark Ray-Ban sunglasses, he hardly appeared to be a race car driver, let alone the most successful one in NASCAR history with seven championships. He was also voted Most Popular Driver nine times by the fans.

Petty amassed 200 race victories, a feat that will never be touched. Carrier told me in the early years of NASCAR, Petty won and dominated so many races because he had STP sponsorship, while other teams struggled to find investors let alone sponsors. Race teams are responsible for the cost of running a race car, including building engines and chassis from scratch and even buying their tires from Goodyear. Traveling across the country from February to November, paying for lodging, food, fuel, etc., for an entire team runs into the hundreds of thousands of dollars.

In December, at the annual NASCAR banquet held at the Waldorf Astoria Hotel in New York City, Petty summoned track officials to outline his plan for his "1992 Fan Appreciation Tour."

Petty unveiled an opportunity for track owners to make some money from a limited edition die-cast replica No. 43 stock car that would have each track's name and logo on it, as well as the date of that particular event.

These small die-cast collectible cars would sell for $10 each with the track receiving a percentage of the profits depending on the number sold. I thought it was a great idea. But Petty's staff wasn't stopping there. There would also be a Richard Petty 1992 Fan Appreciation Tour Decal Collection Series, featuring decals that had been emblazoned on cars Petty had driven, anniversary logos and other decals. A set was $5 and probably cost $1 each to print. You could buy them at all the NASCAR tracks, at his souvenir trailers or you could order them and pay for the shipping. There would also be special hats, T-shirts and a hodgepodge of items in remembrance of "The King."

Upon returning to Bristol, I was approached by Ray Shough, one of our official track photographers and an independent contractor who handled our souvenir sales and set up the souvenir trailers prior to races.

"Hey Ron, you know Petty is going to make a killin' on all those little cars he's going to sell," he said.

"Yeah, so what?" I asked. "I hope he makes a mint. He deserves it for all he's done for the sport and NASCAR."

Shough went on to pitch his idea, suggesting that the track make its own 1:64 scale limited edition collectible die-cast car and pairing it with Petty's souvenir car for $20. Each car would cost $2 to make in China, including shipping, and Shough would receive (I believe) $1. Carrier would net $7 for each collectible sold. We would produce 15,000 for the Food City race in the spring and 15,000 for the Bud 500 in the fall. The track would make $210,000 on the venture.

I convinced Carrier to partner with Shough and on Sunday, April 5, 1992, Bristol International Raceway's Limited Edition Die-Cast Car was unveiled and paired with Richard Petty's collectible. Not surprisingly, we sold most of them and the ones that were left, we stocked at the track's souvenir store. Carrier kept the first five boxes of the numbered cars making the lower numbered collectibles more valuable.

He locked them up in the office closet at the Bristol Sports Arena, located behind the track. He would discover those years later and gave them to family and friends. Today, those "little cars" sell for $20 on eBay. It was quite an opportunity to make a lot of extra cash and now the project is part of BMS track history.

Petty's souvenir die-cast car proved to be popular at all the tracks. Since we sold nearly 15,000 BIR die-cast track cars at both our events, it's hard to tell how many Petty sold at all the NASCAR tracks. We attempted the same project the next year, but sold alone, the track cars just didn't sell very well, so we ended the project of Bristol International Raceway limited edition die-cast cars.

I had Shough put Larry Carrier's name above the door on the BIR die-cast car, as if Carrier were the driver of the car. I was hoping that when Harry Gant announced his retirement, he would have a die-cast track car made and we'd pair ours with his and any other famous driver who retired. But even though most drivers have die-cast souvenir cars, no other retiring driver could pull off what "The King" did. He had a marketing machine and he certainly made the best of the last year he drove. Long live The King!

—

Speaking of making money on souvenir ideas, I was approached by the local post office to turn Bristol International Raceway into a "post office for the day" with our own stamp. It was August 26, 1989, and our post office was called Raceway Station. The self-stamped envelopes featured a sedan from the 1920s.

"I bet you sell a lot of those," said the post office representative. We set up the makeshift post office at the front of the property to attract race fans as they walked in. We had a real U.S. Post Office blue letter receptacle sitting next to a 12-foot table for processing the expected hundreds of cards and letters. For the day, Bristol International Raceway was an official post office with its own ZIP code.

We only sold a dozen envelopes for $1 apiece. We never did that again.

What I thought was another great souvenir idea came from local resident and friend Charlie Arnold, who also was one of our boxing judges. Charlie made knives on the side. In 1993, he developed a Bristol International Raceway limited edition pocketknife that sold for $10 and we received some of the profits from the sale of the knives. I still have knife #2. Charlie, of course, gave Carrier #1.

The Certificate of Authenticity reads:

"To honor Mr. Larry Carrier, owner and President of Bristol International Raceway, this beautiful commemorative knife was created with 'you' the race fan in mind. Being a Special Limited Edition of 1,000, this is sure to become a collectible soon. One blade commemorates a race fan's enthusiasm with the famous term 'Gentlemen Start Your Engines,' while the other blade won't let you forget, 'The World's Fastest Half-Mile.'

I hope you enjoy your commemorative knife and the races at Bristol International Raceway for many years to come."

The knives didn't sell very well, but I thought it was a grand idea and something different from the typical collectibles offered race fans, such as die-cast cars, toy banks and jewelry. Maybe in time, Charlie got rid of the knives. I sure hope so!

CHAPTER 14

The Darkest Day at BIR: Alan Kulwicki is dead

Because of the time of year, I found the April 1993 race weekend aggravating at best. The weather in Northeast Tennessee dictates whether you have a good race weekend – or not. Leading up to Winston Cup race day, I lay awake nights, praying, and I watched the Weather Channel and Bristol television station WCYB around the clock. Larry Carrier never showed the pressure. In fact, he laughed at the weather predictions from local weatherman Dave Dierks from WCYB and admonished me for questioning God's intentions for race weekends.

"Ron, that green flag will drop no matter what you or I do," Larry said. "It always does and there's not a damned thing you can do about it. Fact of the matter is if I could control the weather, I'd be a lot richer than I am right now. These mountains will tell us whether it'll rain or not – not WCYB! The rain will either go over them or not."

Nevertheless, I tried for years to lobby NASCAR to give us a better date. Mike Helton, the president of NASCAR is from Kingsport,

Tenn., 15 miles down the road. He knows better. I wanted another night race date (say, in late September or early October) when I knew the weather would be great and the banging on the high banks would give us two great weekends of racing under the lights at the World's Fastest Half-Mile. Sparks and tempers would flare just like they always did at the August Busch 500. My suggestion was considered but never taken seriously by NASCAR, so in April, we moved on in redundant trepidation.

Enough said. I still had sleepless nights. In racing, as track managers, don't we all?

As was the norm, rather than the exception, the weather for the 1993 Food City 500 was miserable. Rain had set in during the beginning of race week and the first weekend of April wasn't any better. Even though we were sold out for Sunday's Winston Cup Food City 500 race, we always wanted a big crowd for the NASCAR Grand National race on Saturday, because that was where we made our "gravy."

General admission seating for the Busch Beer Grand National race was only $20 a pop, paid at the gate, and we paid only a small purse for the drivers' participation (with many of "big boys" in the field doing what's called "double-duty"). With a reasonable sanctioning fee charged by NASCAR, this situation made for a golden opportunity for racetrack owners to make a lot of money. We also got a nice check from ESPN for the television rights. A good gate at the "little race" also translated into a nice bonus for me and my staff. A bad weather episode kills the deal and makes for an ill track staff. When I looked at the weather forecast for Saturday, I was suddenly both sick and ill.

The weather, however, would soon be the least of my worries and my sleepless nights would turn into a nightmare – literally.

On April 1, on the way to Tri-Cities Regional Airport in Blountville, Tenn., a 15-minute drive to the racetrack, for the Food City 500 weekend, a plane carrying Alan Kulwicki, the defending Winston Cup Series 1992 champion, crashed in a cornfield 10 miles from the airport. Kulwicki was killed, along with four others, in the crash. Ironically, the 38 year-old Kulwicki, was also the defending champion of the Food City 500 race.

He had made an appearance for his primary sponsor at a Hooters restaurant, about 85 miles away in Knoxville, Tenn., on a cold, windy and rainy Thursday evening. Investigators, according to local news reports, later said ice had formed on the plane's wings and visibility was terrible. The 10-passenger twin-engine turboprop lost altitude, disappearing from the airport radar screen, apparently went into a nosedive, crashed and exploded.

I was in my office when the phone began ringing. Larry Carrier was the first to call. He said that he and his two sons, Mark and Andy, were on their way to the crash site.

"You need to stay put. The whole world will be calling you," he said after giving me the details of what little he knew at the time. "All we know is the plane went down and is on fire."

I don't remember what time it was when the call from the first reporter – from *USA Today* – came in to my office, but it was probably about 8 p.m. Once it started, though, the calls kept coming: *The New York Times, Boston Globe, Atlanta Constitution, Nashville Banner, Charlotte Observer* and news organizations from Wisconsin where Alan was from. Every publication that ever covered NASCAR racing called.

As an old newspaperman myself, I remembered feeling weird and somewhat uncomfortable, sitting on the other side of the desk, answering questions as opposed to asking them.

The Darkest Day at BIR: Alan Kulwicki is dead

After fielding the last call, from the British Broadcasting Co. (BBC) in London at 2 a.m. EST, five hours ahead of our time zone, I lay down to sleep on the couch in my office. This tragedy had become an international story. I was exhausted, helpless and dreading what lay before me in the morning.

At 6 a.m., with three hours of sleep, I emerged from my office and drove a golf cart down to the pit area where the race cars sat covered in tarps, protected from the rain. Cold, drizzly rain was falling and a heavy fog had settled over the area. It was darker than normal for that time of year. At about 9 a.m., Kulwicki's transporter made a sad journey around the track backward in the driver's signature "Polish Victory Lap." Moments later, No. 7 was gone and so was the last successful independent racer in NASCAR – gone but never forgotten.

NASCAR Pace Car starter Doyle Ford waved the checked flag as Kulwicki's crew exited the track with the No. 7 race car inside the transporter.

Kulwicki won five races over his Winston Cup career, his first coming at Phoenix in 1988, my first year at Bristol. Although he won a series championship, Bristol was the only track where he had won twice.

In 1992, after his win at the Food City 500 the previous year, I conducted the interview session with all the other reporters in the infield media center.

"How's it feel?" I predictably asked in Victory Lane before his media center visit.

"As compared to what? Next question," he answered with a grin.

Alan Kulwicki Factoid: An underdog from Greenfield, Wisconsin, he produced NASCAR's most unlikely championship run in the

125

1992 NASCAR Winston Cup season. He overcame the greatest late-season deficit in championship history, and along the way gave hope to every small-time operator in NASCAR, which proved to be short-lived.

Kulwicki's 1992 title run proved that hard work, determination, intelligence and some luck can result in a small-time independent operator reaching the pinnacle of the driving profession.

When I remember Alan Kulwicki, I always think about his signature big smile. And, more often than not, that grin would be on a head sticking out from under his race car. He not only drove it, he also worked on it, unlike most NASCAR race car drivers.

By race day, someone came up with the idea of placing No. 7 stickers on all the racecars, and No. 7 patches were worn by everyone associated with the event in remembrance of Kulwicki. Even country music stars Brooks & Dunn, who I had lined up to sing the national anthem, proudly wore the patches. A moment of silence before pre-race activities left nary a dry eye in the house, certainly not in the pit area. No one wanted be there, but as Rusty Wallace said, "Ron, Alan would have wanted us to run today. Just remember that. He was doing what he loved."

Kulwicki's death touched and shocked the entire racing community. Capturing the championship as an independent had won him the adoration of fans across the country and the respect of his fellow drivers.

I also remember Alan as a really smart guy – literally. He's the only race car driver I know who earned an engineering degree (University of Wisconsin, 1977), which I assume assisted him in becoming Winston Cup champion. He knew race cars and could take an engine apart and put back it together again.

Today, we remember Kulwicki as an improbable champion. He never forgot where he came from and enjoyed victory with grace and good humor. He, like Frank Sinatra, did it his way.

At the end of the 1993 Valleydale Meats 500, race winner Rusty Wallace drove his Victory Lap in reverse in honor of his fallen friend. He and other drivers continued the tribute to Kulwicki after other wins throughout the racing season.

Alan Kulwicki was born on December 14, 1954, in Greenfield, Wis. He got his start racing on dirt tracks and dreaming of becoming a racer on the NASCAR Winston Cup Circuit. He eventually graduated from the minor league racing circuits to NASCAR racing. In 1985, he headed South to pursue his NASCAR stock car racing dream. A year later after selling everything he had to "go racing," Alan's dream came true, and with a tight budget, little equipment and skeleton support crew he went on to become Winston Cup Rookie of the Year.

Kulwicki won his first race at Phoenix International Raceway, and he debuted what would become his trademark backward "Polish Victory Lap." Kulwicki won the 1992 Winston Cup championship by what was then the closest margin in NASCAR history. He was chosen one of NASCAR's 50 Greatest Drivers.

He served as driver and crew chief and personally worked on his race car. It's said Junior Johnson tried to get Alan to drive for him but was turned down. Most NASCAR observers said he'd never make it as an independent. He proved them wrong, by winning 24 poles and five races. He won at Phoenix in 1988, Rockingham in 1990, Bristol in 1991 and 1992 and Pocono also in 1992. He came from 278 points behind in the final six races to win the 1992 championship by 10 points, the closest margin in NASCAR history.

CHAPTER 15

Remembering Davey Allison

The sting of Alan Kulwicki's death was not the only sad or fatal story during my time at Bristol International Raceway. The Allisons of Hueytown, Ala., are surely the most tragic family in American motor racing and one of those tragedies occurred during my tenure at the World's Fastest Half-Mile.

As we discussed the dangers and perils of racing stock cars, Davey Allison told me, "Ron, it is a dangerous sport but it's what I love to do. Should I, God forbid, get taken from this world in a race car, I'm gonna go with a smile on my face, knowing I was doing something I loved," he said, summing up his family's acceptance of the "occupational hazard" of stock car racing. But Davey Allison did not suffer that kind of demise. He, like Kulwicki, died in another kind of crash.

Davey Allison was only 32 when he died on July 13, 1993, of massive head injuries he had sustained 16 hours earlier in the crash of a helicopter he was flying. He was attempting to land in a parking lot in the infield of Talladega (Ala.) Superspeedway. That his NASCAR career had seemingly not yet peaked – despite his 19 Winston Cup Series wins, including the 1992 Daytona 500 – was just one of the reasons the nation's racers and fans were so shocked by his death. That he, above all other NASCAR drivers, delighted and influenced children and teenagers with his warm personality and devout life was another reason for mourning.

Even sadder was the fact that Davey was the second of the two sons of former NASCAR star Bobby Allison to die in an accident in the span of 11 months. The preceding August, younger son Clifford Allison, 27, was killed in a stock car crash during practice at the Michigan International Speedway.

The deaths of Bobby Allison's sons came as Bobby, 55, was continuing his own agonizing recovery from a near-fatal, career-ending brain injury suffered in a crash at Pocono (Pa.) International Raceway in 1988. And Bobby's younger brother Donnie, 53, long since retired, raced only sporadically after suffering life-threatening injuries in Charlotte in 1981.

In 1992, Davey Allison had re-evaluated his priorities, especially after a very close call at Pocono, when his car flipped a dozen times. He escaped with a broken right arm and collarbone and a fractured and dislocated wrist, then raced again the next Sunday at his beloved "home track," Talladega Super Speedway.

On the morning after Davey died, Father Dale Grubba reportedly sat staring at his breakfast in a Birmingham motel and wondering, sometimes aloud, what he would say to the Allisons during another time of crisis. For two decades, he had been both a friend and spiritual counselor to the family. At Bristol, Grubba was there, often saying Mass on race Sundays for the Allisons and the handful of other Catholics on the NASCAR tour, including Kulwicki. Grubba conducted Kulwicki's funeral Mass in Milwaukee. And now, on the morning of July 14, 1993, Grubba had flown to Alabama to celebrate Davey Allison's funeral Mass and to comfort, as best he could, the family of the second NASCAR star to die in a private-aircraft crash in just four months.

In 1993, near Bristol International Raceway, the crash that killed Kulwicki and three other people of his staff was still being investigated by the National Transportation Safety Board, and NTSB officials at the time said it would be six months to a year before findings were released on the Allison crash. Semi-retired driver Charles "Red" Farmer, 61, another longtime Allison family friend, was a passenger in the helicopter, but he survived, suffering a broken collarbone and fractured ribs. Farmer and Allison had flown to Talladega from Hueytown, Ala., about 60 miles away, to watch friend Neil Bonnett's son, David, test a car.

According to NTSB investigator Roff Sasser, witnesses reported that Allison's helicopter was within a foot of touching down safely in the parking lot when it began oscillating and suddenly rose about 25 feet into the air. It spun counterclockwise, rolled and crashed, its tail rotor striking a fence on the way down. At the time, no evidence of mechanical failure had been found, but "we've got a long way to go" in examining the wreckage, Sasser said. He would not speculate as to the cause of the crash. Allison, with six years' experience as a pilot of fixed-wing aircraft, reportedly had only about 65 hours of flying time in helicopters and about 10 hours in the Hughes 369-HS that he had bought less than a month before.

Davey's death not only left behind his wife, Liz, and their children, Krista, and Robert, but it also left the larger Allison family without its central pillar. Scarcely an hour after he died, Robert Yates, his car owner, told reporters, "God has asked an awful lot of this family."

Among the many racing people attending the wake and funeral in Alabama – from retired NASCAR driver Benny Parsons to Indy Car and Formula One patriarch Mario Andretti – the question everyone seemed to be asking was, "Why?" Said Andretti in a statement to reporters, "It is beyond my comprehension. If ever there was goodness in anyone, it is in that family – the whole family. They are the example of goodness."

CHAPTER 16

The Sale of Bristol International Raceway

By the end of the 1995 NASCAR Winston Cup season, the sport had exploded. Race teams were picking up million-dollar sponsors. We were getting unimaginable television revenue because of double-digit ratings, and the grandstands were packed by the thousands, from Bristol to Talladega and New York to California.

Life was good and we were letting the good times roll. The August night race at Bristol International Raceway was the most successful in the history of the track, and the most successful in NASCAR racing other than the Daytona 500. It had been voted Track of the Year five straight years by ESPN. Bristol dominated the votes when fans chose their favorite NASCAR racetrack.

Then, for whatever reason, the brakes slammed on.

Believe it or not, Larry Carrier and I had somewhat lost interest in NASCAR and would talk privately about that. The sport seemingly was getting too big to be run as a family-owned business. Whatever was to happen with the track's future, I didn't see myself being a part of. It was pretty much over for me. Looking back on it now, I have no regrets. Time and people move on. As a matter-of-fact I think Larry and I really had become interested in other things and even though we still love the sport of auto racing we saw the changes coming.

We still believed in keeping ticket prices reasonable and we catered to families rather than corporations. Vendors were charged very reasonable prices for parking their souvenir rigs at the front entrance of the race track. I enjoyed seeing moms, dads and the kids walk up to the ticket counter with their favorite driver T-shirts and caps on. That's what the sport was all about. We didn't wear $500 suits and loafers with no socks, as seems to be the norm at some racetracks these days.

I can't lie about being fond of the perks NASCAR offered to track owners and managers but as I said we had other interests, too. Larry enjoyed winning trophies with his champion horses that took center stage on the American Quarter Horse Association circuit and boxing at the Bristol Sports Arena, while I enjoyed traveling all over the world as president of the World Boxing Federation, a sanctioning body Carrier and I started in 1988. Our race weeks only dominated a couple of months of the year, with the rest of the time spent on boxing and horses.

Funny, my mother said one time, "You go to London, England (I had an office there for a time) like I go to Wal-Mart!" I was quite happy with my affiliation with the professional boxing business and still am somewhat active to this day.

The turn of events at Bristol International Raceway began in the summer of 1995 with just one phone call from Bruton Smith, a self-made billionaire and owner of a bevy of NASCAR tracks including Charlotte Motor Speedway, Texas Motor Speedway and Las Vegas Motor Speedway.

It was a bright, summer afternoon when Larry called and told me to pick him up for lunch outside our quaint office building. The offices were just a few yards from Volunteer Parkway, the "main drag" that takes you to downtown Bristol and connects to Interstate 81 into Virginia. The call wasn't unusual because we ate lunch together most every day of the week. In fact, if you wanted to find either one of us at lunchtime, we were generally manning a booth at the Bonfire Restaurant, (now unfortunately closed) four miles up the Parkway.

I had barely settled into my seat in Larry's new red Ford Tahoe when the discussion began about a phone call he'd received earlier from Bruton Smith. Larry conveyed the conversation:

"This is Bruton Smith and I wanted to buy your racetrack," Carrier retold. "I said, 'Really? That's funny because it's not for sale.'

"Well, just think about it and how much you'd have to have and I'll call you back in a few days. I think it would be worth investigating," Smith told Carrier.

"Well, you can call back but it's not for sale," Carrier said.

My reaction was an eloquent, "Wow!" followed by a question, "How does one put a price on a racetrack?" And, not just any old racetrack but THE World's Fastest Half-Mile?

"Doesn't matter," Carrier said. "We ain't selling."

The drive to the Bonfire was a silent one except for the hum of the air-conditioning through the front dashboard vents. My mind was traveling a mile a minute and I imagined that his was, too.

Surprisingly, we didn't talk anymore about the phone call because at lunchtime we were always interrupted by people with questions for Larry about last Sunday's race or if there were any tickets left and 'How do you get an autograph of so-and-so?' and 'How much is a pit pass?' and 'Is this or that driver a nice guy?' – and on and on. Larry would take each question and answer it the best he knew how between bites from his vegetable plate, which he ordered day-in and day-out.

Even though he avoided the limelight and it was difficult for me, as his PR man, to push him center stage, I could tell Larry enjoyed these lunchtime sessions that regularly lasted two hours or more every day. He had garnered the respect of his peers and, at the same time, had remained grounded.

I looked up to Larry, not only as a boss and mentor, but also as a father figure. We viewed things similarly and during my employment there, we never had a heated disagreement, although there were spirited discussions from time-to-time. That was just the nature of our business. Some people said Larry could be difficult at times. I never saw that.

Back at the office came what I would later label as "The Meeting." It was Larry and members of his immediate family and I. There was no agenda or formal presentation. It was just a good ol' discussion about the benefits of selling the track – or not.

An hour into the discussion, Larry looked my way and asked THE question: "Ron, what do you think?"

It was one of those, "You could cut the silence with a knife moments."

I thought it was awesome that I'd even been invited to this meeting. After all, I was an employee of 10 years, not an owner and certainly not a member of the family, but still I guess when you are involved in the daily operations for that long, your opinion and expertise mean something.

"So, here goes," I thought to myself and began searching for my bottle of water to wet my parched throat. "Well, I personally think you're in the throes of major changes within NASCAR and the sport of racing in general, but I'm not telling you anything you don't already know. There are good and bad things associated with Bruton's proposal.

"No. 1: This is not about Bristol International Raceway. This is about your race dates. I use the term 'your' very loosely because NASCAR controls the dates. You don't own them. I'm no lawyer however it seems to me it would be difficult for NASCAR to pull a date from you. Because, let's face it, you were there when they needed you as much as you needed them in building up the sport. And, look at your record; your race events have been selling out for decades, spring and fall. Hell, I couldn't get a ticket unless I was the general manager. And, every time I look up you are adding more seats!

"No. 2: NASCAR can and the fans will demand more seats, more amenities, and an expanded infrastructure will be needed to make that happen. Who knows what ESPN is going to want? NASCAR's sanctioning fee will probably double, as will the purse for the drivers.

"No. 3: With regards to No. 2, we are probably looking at a minimum investment cost of $7 million right now and upwards of $10 million in track expansion for seating and all those other amenities. You've got to ask yourself if you want to make that type of commitment and at what risk."

I wasn't done. "Also," I said, "I'm really worried about the Food City 500. Speaking of dates, remember when the Valleydale 500 was on

April 9? Now the spring race is the first weekend in the month but I'm hearing it could be moved into March as the schedule expands. As you know, our spring event is no kin to the Busch 500. In the spring, fans come to the races, get in their cars when it's over and they are gone. We don't have a clue if it's going to rain or snow. The night race, on the other hand, is a weeklong party. People are on vacation. They camp here for a week. Our souvenir sales are double. We don't sleep for days. [Everyone laughed.] Also, can we sell 100,000 seats for the Food City 500 race versus 70,000? I don't know about that. We can in the fall, I'm certain. But, are we going to be able to take care of another 30,000 race fans? Hell, you can't get a room now between Bristol and Asheville! And, think about the traffic coming in and out of the track. It takes us five to six hours now to get everyone out after a race, which in itself is some kind of miracle.

"I guess you have to ask yourself personally at this time in your lives, do you want to continue to do this? Honestly, it seems to me that Mark's interest is with professional boxing and NHRA drag racing, and Andy is an accomplished AQHA horseman at the highest level. The WBF is to the point that I'm being invited to stage events in countries that I can't even pronounce. And that's another good thing you started, Larry Carrier.

"And I might be talking myself out of a job, but if it's a big enough number … I say, 'Sell it.' You're in the outdoor entertainment business. NASCAR is at the height of popularity, but have you seen how many kids are kicking a soccer ball around these days? The economy is great right now but that could also change, as you experienced in the past. Remember gas rationing?

"Whatever you want to do, I'm with you 100 percent and I say, 'Full steam ahead.' Either way, it's been a great ride, hasn't it?"

The sale between Carrier and Smith was official in January 1996. Later that year, Smith purchased a half-interest in the historic North Wilkesboro Speedway with Bob Bahre. This speedway was the first to hold a NASCAR race and was a popular track with many fans because of its history and the short track, which provided many chances for the "bumping and banging" associated with the early days of the sport.

However, Smith and Bahre created a controversy when, citing North Wilkesboro Speedway's age, lack of modern amenities and relatively small stadium area, they decided to transfer its two Winston Cup events to Bahre's New Hampshire International Speedway and Smith's Texas Motor Speedway. This move came under criticism from many NASCAR traditionalists, who felt that Smith was moving NASCAR away from its small-town roots in North Carolina. Critics of the decision also felt Smith was slighting smaller-venue short tracks – which traditionalists believe better reflect the history of the sport – in favor of the large tracks that allow more fans but provide a less-intimate fan experience.

The process of moving NASCAR races away from smaller-but-historic tracks in the small-town South to much larger tracks nationwide continues to be a source of controversy.

Promoting NASCAR racing had become as a big a business as the NFL, Major League Baseball and the NBA. I don't blame Bruton Smith or the other promoters however, what started as a run down the beach at Daytona, Fla., in 1947 has ended in a run for some of the biggest bucks in international sports.

Interesting Factoids about BMS:

1. In his last racing event as General Manager, Ron Scalf observed Dale Earnhardt Sr. literally run over Terry Labonte at the start-finish line on the last lap at the Busch 500 in 1995 almost taking the checkered flag. It was the closest finish ever recorded at Bristol.
Until Earnhardt did the same thing the next year.

2. Michael Waltrip's spectacular crash into the Turn 2 cross-over gate during a Busch Grand National Race remains the most horrific crash in BMS history. His car is on display in the Hall of Fame. On the day of the sale, the local media were all treated to a steak dinner not knowing management was about to change forever.

3. Carrier took some of the sales proceeds to purchase Tri-Cities Golf Course, located near the track which his family owns and manages today.

4. In the 1990s, Carrier turned down an offer of $9 million to move the races to Newport, Tennessee where a new [proposed] superspeedway would be built.

5. The University of Tennessee Volunteer vs. Virginia Tech Hokie football team contest at the Speedway will set attendance records for years to come.

Acknowledgments

Today, Ron Scalf works in a management position with the Savannah, Ga. Tourism Leadership Council. After leaving Bristol Motor Speedway, he continued as president of the World Boxing Federation another eight years. He has an adult son, Tyler, who lives in Nashville and a 10-year-old Maltese (adopted from an animal shelter in North Carolina) named Snoopy.

Lise Cutshaw, an editor, educator and PR professional at East Tennessee State University served as copy editor for "Racin' The Way It Was."

Ron wishes to thank track photographers, Ray Shough, John Beach and David Chobat, as well as Andy, Shirley and Mark Carrier and former track co-owner Carl Moore for their contributions to this book.

Made in United States
Orlando, FL
29 August 2023